THE REAL YOU
FULLY ALIVE

Spirit Soul Body

Jeff Klingenberg

Renown Publishing
www.renownpublishing.com

The Real You Fully Alive / Jeff Klingenberg
ISBN-13: 978-1-960236-16-6

PRAISE FOR AUTHOR JEFF KLINGENBERG AND *THE REAL YOU FULLY ALIVE*

This book can help you discover the keys to spiritual alignment and abundant living. "The Real You: Fully Alive" by my friend, Jeff Klingenberg is filled with deep insights and practical guidance. This book is designed to equip readers to align their spirit, soul, and body with God's purpose. Through biblical wisdom and personal anecdotes, Jeff offers tangible steps on how to nurture your physical body, renew your mind, and experience the fullness of God's blessings.

Michael, Jr., Stand Up Comedian and Author of *Funny How Life Works*

The issue of identity is a central issue that is facing this generation in a way that perhaps it never has. Who are we *really* and how should we then live that truth out in real time. In this outstanding new book, *The Real You: Fully Alive*, my friend Jeff Klingenberg parses out what it means to be a new creation in Christ and the battle that takes place to walk in the fullness of that reality. I can't think of anyone more qualified to write on this subject than a long tenured shepherd, who has taught and led countless people down the path of walking in the fullness of "In Christ". I promise you, this book will bless you!

Lee Cummings, Senior Leader of Radiant Church and Radiant Network of Churches and Author of *Take Heed, Watch and Pray* and *School of the Spirit*

I have known Pastor Jeff for more than two decades and his steadfastness, wisdom and spiritual insight have been powerfully consistent. What you read in this much needed book has been birthed from a life well lived as a husband, father, pastor, and friend.

Brady Boyd, Senior Pastor of New Life Church and Author of *Remarkable, Speak Life, Fear No Evil, Addicted to Busy, Let Her Lead, Sons & Daughters,* **and** *Extravagant*

Pastor Jeff Klingenberg's book, *The Real You—Fully Alive* is an excellent road map to help us discover and celebrate our true selves in Jesus. Practical, biblical, accessible, and helpful are words that come to mind to describe this important book. The Apostle Paul exhorts believers to know (regard) no man according to the flesh but rather see each other the way the Holy Spirit sees us. (2 Cor. 5:16–17) My friend Pastor Jeff has given the reader tools to help us see ourselves and others the way God sees us.

E. Wayne Drain, Founding Pastor of City Church, President of Wayne Drain Ministries, and Author of *He Still Speaks*

It has been my joy to know Jeff Klingenberg for over twenty years, as a pastor, teacher, leader, and friend. Jeff shares from his experiences how to live in your true identity as a Spirit-led being in a non-spirit-led world. The most important thing we can discover is who we are in Christ and how to live daily in a world that does not embrace the spiritual life. No matter where you are on your spiritual journey, the truths in this book, *The Real You: Fully Alive*, will inspire you, help you, guide your thinking, reveal some lies you may have embraced, and remind you who you really are in God's eyes so that you can live completely free to be who God intended for you to be. I wholeheartedly recommend this book.

Tom Lane, Author and Founder of The Executive Leadership Institute

Pastor Jeff Klingenberg's unwavering commitment to strengthening people for life shines through in this transformative book, an embodiment of his life's mission. By harnessing the timeless wisdom of God's Word, this book offers a path to profound strength across all facets of a believer's life. In a world where chaotic emotions, unhealthy habits and dysfunction often prevail, Pastor Jeff's insights challenge us to rethink our approach and embrace holistic health rooted in biblical truth. In this book, we discover that the journey to a healthy soul, spirit, and body is not just possible but essential for living a vibrant, faith-filled life brimming with purpose. Each chapter seamlessly blends deep spiritual insights with practical applications, paving the way for true strength and enduring transformation.

Tim Ingram, Senior Pastor of HighRidge Longview, President of Unite Leadership, and Author of *Greater Than: Discovering the Things That Keep Us from God's Best* and *7 Things That Keep Us from God's Best: Discovering the God Who Is Greater Than the Modern-Day Idols in Our Lives*

The title of this book says it all—*The Real You Fully Alive*. I can personally attest to the transformative wisdom contained in this book. Having served as a staff pastor at HighRidge Church and now serving as a Senior Pastor, my life has been deeply impacted by Pastor Jeff's teaching on the spirit, soul, and body. There simply is no other book like this out there. Pastor Jeff masterfully leads the reader through a compelling, biblical, and insightful journey to discover who God created us to be and how that fact positively impacts our lives. This book is a resource for anyone looking to live out their God-given potential—fully alive.

Tim Rivers, D.Ed.Min, Senior Pastor, Embassy City Church

I dedicate this book to my Lord and Savior, Jesus Christ, to my dynamic and supportive wife, Dawn, and to my wonderful children, their spouses, and my grandchildren.

I also dedicate this to my spiritual family at HighRidge Church, who have been so effective at receiving these teachings and helping them get even better.

CONTENTS

Who Is the Real You?

Do you have trouble with your thoughts? Fear? Condemnation? Rejection? Do you linger over decisions to the point of frustration? Do you find yourself wondering why you responded to someone the way you did? I wrote this book for you!

What would you think if I told you that you aren't who you think you are? Would you believe me if I said that your life could be much better than it currently is? Imagine having a deep river of meaningful abundance flowing through each and every day and all of those days being virtually free from setbacks. On top of this, you could live with an overflowing measure of peace and a full understanding that you are much more like your divine Creator than you previously realized.

The purpose of this book is to help you realize who you really are and how to become fully alive. Most people go about their daily lives, failing to realize they are not fully alive as God has designed them to be. It is God's desire for you to have what the Bible calls "abundant life." Experiencing that abundant life starts by asking yourself, *Who am I, really?* It's a question that is important to answer, and it's even more crucial to accept the answer fully. Once you understand who you are and your position in this life, you will be better able to face whatever life throws your way, and that abundant life will be yours for the living.

When I talk about this concept of identity and its vital importance in helping us reach our full potential and stay strong through some of life's hardest challenges, I mean it. I have lived it. This concept was never more significant to me than when I faced one of the greatest health challenges of my life in 2018. I will never forget this date, April 13th, 2018, when I experienced what my family and I now call "the event."

After years of suffering through allergies and taking allergy medication to survive the harsh Texas springs and unforgiving winters, my prostate had taken the brunt of the abuse. I never knew that taking allergy medication consistently can have severe consequences for men because it can affect the rate a male's prostate becomes enlarged over time. The symptoms of this condition were interrupting my rest cycles at night, but also were affecting my ability to enjoy the one thing that I love most: teaching the Word of God each Sunday at HighRidge Church. Just enduring through a single message was a challenge, and we have multiple services each week. With this and other growing concerns, doctors suggested I take steps to reduce the prostate and protect my health.

After praying for wisdom, researching diligently,

obtaining wise counsel, and carefully seeking God's guidance, I decided to go in for a procedure that would laser the
tissue that was causing the issue. I went in on Friday after-
noon, April 13th, for an outpatient procedure that should
have only taken about an hour. But I did not leave the hospi-
tal until 2 weeks later, and during that time, doctors were
uncertain if I would leave at all.

While under anesthesia, complications occurred causing
my bladder to rupture, forcing my body to shut down my
kidneys, redirecting all fluids flowing through my body to be
absorbed back in through the retroperitoneum. When my
kidneys shut down, a message was sent to my brain that my
body was dying. In an effort to save my life, my brain initiated
a process called rhabdomyolysis, which began to deteriorate
several muscles in my body. All this happened Friday after-
noon, but I did not regain full consciousness until sometime
between Monday night and early Tuesday morning. As I
came back from a medically-induced coma, I awakened to
more pain than I had ever experienced in my life. I learned
that at one point during the days prior I was only hours away
from dying, that my kidneys had completely failed, and I had
a long road of recovery ahead of me. As I faced this life-defin-
ing crisis and the arduous path of recovery ahead, it was my
understanding of my true identity, the very truth I am passing to you in the pages ahead, that I returned to strength and
vitality.

In this book, we're going to dig into the self-discovery process and identify *who* you are in the eyes of God and *whose*
you are as His child. You are a son or daughter of the Most

High. You have been bought with a price you could not pay, covering every debt you could ever owe, because that's how much your heavenly Father wants a relationship with you. That's how much He wants to bless your life with abundance. To help you embrace this truth fully, we'll also look at how to live a godly and abundant life in every part of your being—spirit, soul, and body.

God loves you so much that He wants you to claim every privilege that comes with belonging to Him. In the process, He wants to make you more like Him. The more you allow Him to mold you into His image, the more you can enjoy all the richness of His love and favor that comes with being a co-heir with Christ.

Right now, you are in the process of being molded, shaped, and formed by God. The Creator of the heavens and the earth—the one who forever has been, is now, and forever will be—loves you so deeply that He wants to help you live a blessed and abundant life. He knows exactly what needs to change and grow in you for you to embrace that life fully. He knows who you are, and that you belong to Him.

This is much more than a book about your identity in Christ; this is a journey to self-discovery that starts with believing and receiving the titles of honor given to you by God, who is the King of kings. You are a priest and a king (Revelation 1:6). You are royalty (1 Peter 2:9). You're an overcomer (Romans 8:37). These identifying markers create the starting line toward a blessed life by revealing *who* you are and *whose* you are.

To grasp our true identity, we must understand that we

are holistic beings made in the image of God. Our existence is made up of three parts: spirit, soul, and body. By examining what is available in each of these parts, we can more fully understand how to step into the life that God offers and desires for us to experience.

The message of this book comes from the following verse:

> *Now may the God of peace Himself sanctify you completely; and may your whole spirit, soul, and body be preserved blameless at the coming of our Lord Jesus Christ.*
>
> **—1 Thessalonians 5:23**

Too many people are living their lives according to their feelings, emotions, moods, and the impulses of their bodies. This shows a limited understanding of how human beings really work. As Christians, we should tune in to the Spirit every day, in all aspects of our lives. When we do, the pieces of our lives will naturally fall into their proper places.

This book digs into the details of our triune existence and how it relates to a Spirit-led life. The Spirit-led life is a blessed life, one that we were created to live to the fullest extent. Together, we'll explore how your spirit should lead the way and how your soul and body should follow.

The goal of all of this is to help you walk in the abundance of God's grace. When you understand *who* you really are and *whose* you really are, you are in a position to be molded by God and to step into the abundant life Jesus came to give you.

I have come that they may have life, and that they may have it more abundantly.

—John 10:10

Let's start by asking ourselves, *Who am I, really?*

CHAPTER ONE

We Are Triune Beings

The Creator who made us is actually three distinct persons in one: God the Father, God the Son, and God the Holy Spirit. Do you live your life as the God-mirror that you were created to be? We are each created with a spirit, a soul, and a body—an image of the Trinity—but do you live with these three aspects of your being in their proper order? Does your spirit take the lead, or does it sometimes seem like your body or your emotions are driving the bus?

To understand who we are, we must first understand more about the God who made us in His image, what it takes to become like Him, and how to be saved from the enemy who wants to sabotage that process.

I remember being in seminary and not understanding the concept of God in three persons. Then, one day, a fellow seminary student asked our professor, "How can we understand the Trinity?"

The professor's reply clarified the theology for me in a

THE REAL YOU FULLY ALIVE

brilliant, memorable way. "It's pretty simple," he said. "The easiest analogy to understand the Trinity is H_2O."

When H_2O isn't freezing or boiling, it's water. When H_2O is 212 degrees Fahrenheit or above, it's steam. When H_2O is 32 degrees or below, it's ice. No matter what form H_2O takes—a solid (ice), a liquid (water), or a gas (vapor)—it's still H_2O.

We can think of these three forms as representing the Trinity, with God the Father as water. God the Son is like ice, as He is God in solid form. That leaves God the Holy Spirit, who is like steam.

Isn't it amazing that God chose to reveal Himself in three persons? And He didn't stop there. God made human beings triune, like He is, but instead of being three persons or beings in one, we are three parts in one person: spirit, soul, and body.

Let's dive into some scriptures that address our three-in-one makeup:

> *Now may the God of peace Himself sanctify you completely; and may your whole spirit, soul, and body be preserved blameless at the coming of our Lord Jesus Christ. He who calls you is faithful, who also will do it.*
>
> **—1 Thessalonians 5:23–24**

The Holy Spirit authored these verses through the pen of the Apostle Paul. Paul wrote this church letter while in prison so he could teach the people of Thessalonica profound truths about their identity that they hadn't yet fully grasped.

Here, Paul referenced the "God of peace Himself," which is reflexive language. "Himself" refers back to God.

2

Whenever this kind of wording appears in the Bible, it's a point of emphasis. It's like saying, "Hey, everybody, pay attention. God Himself has something to say."

In this text, *sanctify* means "to make holy." If you're sanctified, it means that you have been made holy before God. This doesn't mean immediate perfection; it's a process of *becoming*.

Now, I have good news for you. God loves you so much that He doesn't want to leave you to tackle the tough, ongoing sanctification process alone. He wants to work in your life to make it more like His. Why? Because He knows that His life is the best, most blessed life to live, and He wants you to benefit from living it. That's why He is in the process of making you holy. God knows that you're a work in process, and, one day you will be whole ("sanctify you completely").

Pay particular attention to how the above scripture refers to "spirit, soul, and body." The Greek word for *spirit* in this context is *pneuma*. It literally means "to be with breath, wind, or gas."[1] What is your *pneuma*? It's the Holy Spirit.

The Greek word for *soul* here is *psyche*,[2] which has three parts as well: mind, will, and emotions. Your soul is your total personality. It's who you *think* you are, but it's not who you *really* are.

In this text, the word *body* is the Greek word *soma*.[3] Your *soma* is your entire collection of cells—your earth suit, if you will.

The point is that God wants every part of you to be made holy. He wants your life to be so abundantly blessed that it mimics His life, and He wants your spirit, soul, and body to

3

be blameless when Christ returns.

To understand how we can grab hold of this blameless life, we need to take another look at verse 24:

He who calls you is faithful, who also will do it.

—1 Thessalonians 5:24

Aren't you glad that we have a faithful God? He is not a part-time God; He is an all-the-time God. Our God is full of faith. He doesn't sometimes doubt you and sometimes believe in you. The way He feels toward you doesn't change based on how you feel about yourself.

Now let's look at the second part of verse 24: "who also will do it." God is the one who will sanctify you and, if you will let Him, work abundance in your life.

Before we jump into the next scripture, let's recall what we discussed at the beginning of this chapter: God in the three persons of Father, Son, and Holy Spirit and you having three parts. The three parts of a human being—spirit, soul, and body—are mentioned in the following verse as well:

For the word of God is living and powerful, and sharper than any two-edged sword, piercing even to the division of soul and spirit, and of joints and marrow, and is a discerner of the thoughts and intents of the heart.

—Hebrews 4:12

I love the Word of God! It's powerful, effective, and sharper than a sword. Wherever the Word of God goes, it has a profound effect.

When reading verses like these, it's easy to see why some people think that the spirit and the soul are the same thing or that they merge once we're saved, but that's not how it works. The spirit and the soul are not, and never become, one thing. Not only are they two different words, but they're treated in two different ways in Scripture. As I mentioned above, the Greek word for *spirit* is *pneuma*, and the Greek word for *soul* is *psyche*. In the Bible, these words are never used interchangeably, and never does one represent the other.

Let's take a closer look at the "thoughts and intents of the heart" portion of this verse. The word *thoughts* refers to your mind and perceptions. The word *intents* refers to your will and purpose and how you make decisions. The word *heart* refers to your emotions and feelings. When we put it all together, "thoughts and intents of the heart" encompass your mind and perceptions, your will and purpose, and your emotions and feelings.

What am I getting at here? I'm describing your personality. I'm describing how you think, make decisions, and respond to the world. I'm also describing how you're known. In other words, I'm painting a picture of who you probably *think* you are.

As followers of Christ, we need to understand that the soul—the mind, will, and emotions—is where spiritual warfare is the most prominent. Have you ever had a random evil thought pop into your mind and wondered where in the world—or, more accurately, where in the pits of hell—did that thought come from? Often the thoughts that pop into our heads come directly from our enemy.

I once dated a girl, albeit for a very short time, who just so happened to be a redhead. When on a date once, I asked if a stop at McDonald's would be okay with her. She immediately yelled at me, "I hate McDonald's and can't believe you would think of me that lowly!" After a brief pause of awkward silence while I tried to figure out what I had done wrong (ladies, it's a place we frequently dwell as men—bewilderment about what we did wrong), she said, "I'm just a redheaded gal, and I say it like I see it." That emotional outburst due to a physical attribute is not who she really was. She had accepted something into her life that was soulish and not spiritual.

Think about it. How do those ungodly thoughts enter our minds? It happens because the enemy knows how to get into our lives and break us down. He is always shooting thoughts, like arrows, into our minds, trying to get us to respond from our souls. The enemy doesn't want us to respond from our spirit, the part of us that is directly connected to the indwelling presence of God. If we fail to respond from our connection to God, we stay open to spiritual attack. That's why the human mind is where the enemy chooses to wage war.

If we haven't made the Spirit of God dominant in our lives, our minds, will, and emotions will often lose the battles. The enemy is on the prowl, looking for every opportunity to sabotage our advances in becoming more holy, more like God. We can thwart these schemes! We can be saved in every part of our being and win every battle.

EVERY PART OF YOU IS SAVED

When you believe in Jesus Christ as the Son of God and receive Him as your Lord and Savior, your salvation occurs in the past, present, and future and encompasses all parts of your triune being.

You *have been saved* by the blood of Christ. That's your spiritual salvation. When you were saved, the Spirit of God set up His throne within you, sealing you forever. Your name is in God's heavenly book of life, and eternal life with our almighty God is waiting for you.

Presently, you *are being saved* in the ongoing sanctification process. This is the salvation of your soul. The Bible says to "work out your own salvation with fear and trembling" (Philippians 2:12). Why would you need to do that if you were made perfect at the moment of salvation? Sometimes ungodly thoughts take over, shoving godly thoughts to the background and prompting emotional responses. You mistakenly think, *It's okay. That's just the way I am.* Those thoughts that don't yield to the indwelling Spirit pollute your soul and need cleaning out. This aspect of salvation is ongoing and will be needed for as long as you're in this fallen world.

Finally, in the future, you *will be saved*. This is the salvation of your body. Someday, your earthly body will be transformed into a perfect heavenly body.

We have been saved (spirit), we are being saved (soul), and we will be saved (body). We are made in the image of a faithful God who is in the process of making us holy. He has given us everything we need to live Spirit-led lives.

To begin exploring the power and beauty of this truth, think about the fairy tale of Cinderella. When that young lady showed up at the royal ball, nobody suspected that she had lived in poverty her entire life and worked as a maid. Everyone at the ball thought she was a princess, and rightly so. See, before arriving, she had been given everything she needed: a fancy dress, gorgeous shoes, beautifully coiffed hair, and an immaculate carriage with a driver, attendants, and horses. If just one of those things had been left out, the royal guards and everyone at the ball would have suspected Cinderella of being someone else. Yet, because everything was right—at least until the stroke of midnight—she embodied who she said she was.

Like Cinderella, who was given everything she needed to be a princess, you have been given everything you need to live as royalty, to live a Spirit-led life. However, it's not always easy to let the Spirit lead. Often the soul or the body hops into the driver's seat. When that happens, problems follow. We need to make sure that God's grace touches every aspect of our being: spirit, soul, and body. Otherwise, things just aren't right!

There are all too many real-life examples within the church. A Christian man I know (whom I'll call Henry) was, by all external appearances, a man who loved God with all his heart, soul, and mind. What no one could see was that, time and again, he chose to cultivate loneliness in his soul by frequenting pornography. It was a dark and hidden sin that he thought he could master and keep secret. The Spirit of God was not in control, so Henry's emotions and body took over his life. His spirit sat in the back seat, unable to wield any power, while sin had its way with a child of God.

Another example is a Christian woman I knew decades ago, whom I'll call Andrea. Andrea put an Ichabod curse on her pastor (we'll call him Carson). An Ichabod curse is a departure of the glory of God (1 Samuel 4:21–22). Consider what it would mean for God to leave you. It's inconceivable, right? It would be absolutely horrible to lose the glory of God, and that is what Andrea wanted Carson to experience. At the same time, Andrea was working as a bookkeeper and stealing money from her employer, all while being identified as a Christian.

It came as quite a shock to Carson when he eventually found out. He had previously known Andrea only as she presented herself: a strong Christian woman who was active in women's ministries and always talking about what the Lord told her. She was presenting "a form of godliness" while sinning every day at her job (2 Timothy 3:5), yet she felt the need to lash out at a pastor who had done nothing wrong to her. Andrea thought that the Holy Spirit was leading her to curse Carson, but she was deceived. The Holy Spirit wasn't calling the shots in her life. Andrea was ignoring the poor health of her own spirit, which left an opening for her emotions to step up as the boss.

With Henry and Andrea, something was clearly amiss. Their souls, not their spirits, were leading the way. To illuminate this subtle yet instrumental distinction, we'll examine three statements regarding our nature as triune beings:

I am a spiritual being.

I possess a soul.

I live in a body.

These three statements provide a straightforward framework for understanding what the Holy Spirit spoke through the Apostle Paul in First Thessalonians and through whomever wrote Hebrews (I think it was Barnabas or Silas, but that's beside the point). In the passages that mention the spirit, the soul, and the body, the Holy Spirit lets us know how these three parts are supposed to work together in each human being.

We tend to focus on the here and now: *How do I feel? What do I need? What will make me happy right now?* We forget that our actions today have consequences. We forget that, to live a blessed and abundant life, we must lean into the Spirit and toward what's perfectly real. The earthly realm, while mirroring reality, is not *perfectly* real, because it's tainted by sin and darkness.

Despite the broken near-reality around us, we can possess a mindset that will both open us up to a blessed life now and prepare us for eternity. Let's explore the three statements that will help us to establish and maintain this mindset.

STATEMENT #1: I AM A SPIRITUAL BEING

When we say, "I am a spiritual being," what does that mean? I once heard a pastor say that the spirit within a Christian is the ruling faculty that allows him or her to interact with the unseen world. The moment you trust Christ, your spirit is saved, brought to life, and destined to be with God for eternity. However, you still lack a practical awareness of the unseen world. It's the Spirit of God that allows you to recognize what isn't seen, like God Himself.

Have you ever had an overwhelming awareness of the greatness and goodness of God during worship? If so, then it happened because the Holy Spirit stirred you and heightened your consciousness, allowing you to engage with the unseen world where God dwells.

If you don't have Christ as your Savior and the Spirit of God within you, then you can't understand what God's presence in your life is like. You can't envision where Jesus sits and where God is. You can't grasp the idea of the heavenly host praising Him and declaring, "Holy, holy, holy is the LORD of hosts; the whole earth is full of His glory!" (Isaiah 6:3).

You can't comprehend these things if you don't yet have the Spirit. In order to begin living life in the Spirit, you need to allow God to do for you what you can't do for yourself: forgive your sins. Jesus came to the earth, lived a sinless life, and died a sacrificial death. He conquered sin, death, and the grave because He loves you. Jesus wants to help you break out of your difficulties. He wants you to have access to His help and His abundant life.

> *And if Christ is in you, the body is dead because of sin, but the Spirit is life because of righteousness.*
>
> **—Romans 8:10**

Reading English in the twenty-first century, we see the word *if* and think it's setting a condition, but that wasn't necessarily the case in the past—including thousands of years ago, when people were speaking ancient Greek. *If* could be interchangeable with *since* in some instances.[4] Thus, "if Christ is in you, the body is dead" may be read as "since Christ is in you, the body is dead." Simply put, your body doesn't have to call the shots; the indwelling Spirit can.

Now let's consider the next verse in Romans:

> *But if the Spirit of Him who raised Jesus from the dead dwells in you, He who raised Christ from the dead will also give life to your mortal bodies through His Spirit who dwells in you.*
>
> **—Romans 8:11**

The Spirit of God dwells in you, beginning at the moment of salvation, and gives life to your mortal body. For me, this happened at nine years old. The church that I grew up in had a revival service twice a year, one in the spring and one in the fall. During one of these revival services, an evangelist preached about how to be saved. At the end of the service, he said, "I'm going to pray right now that those of you who don't know Jesus as your Savior won't be able to fall asleep tonight until you receive Him as your Savior."

That took hold of my nine-year-old mind. I went to bed that night, and I couldn't fall asleep! I was crying; I was tormented. I knew that I wasn't going to be with Christ in His heaven forever.

I asked my mom, "What can I do?"

"You're under conviction," she said. "Pray with me."

I prayed and received Christ. At that moment, my body became a temple of the Holy Spirit. My name was sealed in God's book of life, the book of names in heaven (Revelation 20:15).

I had received Jesus as my Savior, but I had not yet received the Spirit, as Jesus asked each of us to do. As I was growing and learning about this, I discovered a difference between people who had religion and those who had a relationship. The best way for me to illustrate this difference is through the following scripture:

> The spirit of a man is the lamp of the LORD, searching all the inner depths of his heart.
> **—Proverbs 20:27**

From age nine to age twenty, I had a dim lamp. The light didn't glow very brightly within me. I tried to be good enough, but all of that effort wore me out. I had a hard time being good.

While I knew that my eternal life with God was secure, I wasn't living by the Spirit. I was losing many spiritual battles.

Then, when I was twenty, I met a bunch of people who loved Jesus in a way I'd never seen before. After meeting them, I realized how dim my lamp was compared to theirs, which shone brilliantly.

The group I'm referring to is what many people back then called the *Jesus people*. They came to my hometown, loving God, loving to worship Him, and always wearing smiles on their faces.

They were former hippies who had found God, and they were unlike anyone I had seen before. They drove Volkswagen vans with flowers painted on the side, played acoustic guitars, and wore tie-dyed T-shirts and bell-bottom jeans. Their hair was long and messy, and, pew, their hygiene was questionable!

If you'll pardon an overused word from the 1960s, their whole *vibe* was different. When they sang, worshipped, and prayed, it gave me goosebumps. Their voices were like a harmony of angels that lifted my spirit higher with every note. As their melody echoed through the hall, it was almost as if time itself slowed down to listen to their song. Their words, filled with reverence and devotion, made me feel connected to something greater than myself.

I thought, *I've never seen this before. There's got to be something wrong with this.* Soon I realized that *I* was wrong.

The difference was that they had made the choice to receive the Holy Spirit. I was missing something, so I asked them to pray for me. When they did, the glow in me changed. My mindset also changed. I started to think a different way, which led me to start living a different way.

Later, I learned that what had happened to me had also happened to other people. In Acts 19, the disciples met a group of people in Ephesus who were living according to the teachings of the Scriptures and had received John's baptism. The disciples asked these people, "Did you receive the Spirit?"

They replied, "What Spirit? We haven't even heard that there is a Spirit."

In today's world, many churches seldom talk about the Holy Spirit. They place more emphasis on other aspects of our faith. Perhaps some church leaders have a lack of understanding about the Holy Spirit and find it challenging to articulate His role in a way that's relatable to their congregation. Others may be hesitant to talk about the Holy Spirit due to a fear of causing division or controversy within the church.

Whatever the reason, it's essential to note that, while some churches may not talk much about the Holy Spirit, He is a fundamental part of our faith. It is our spirit, united with His, that should lead the way in life, not our emotions or desires.

We shouldn't live from offense to offense, from frustration to frustration. That's not the life God has for us. God offers a blessed and abundant life, but He didn't create us to be robots. We have to make the choice and decide for ourselves the kind of life we're going to live.

I'm here to tell you that a life lived with the Spirit of God calling the shots is a blessed way to live. It is an awesome way to live.

STATEMENT #2: I POSSESS A SOUL

Did you know that the soul is the center of the personality? Your mind, will, and emotions—the three parts of your soul—come together to make up what people know about you. That's who they *think* you are, but it's not who you really are. You are a Spirit-led child of God with the capacity and opportunity to live an abundant life.

While you may value other people's opinions of you, it's important to note that these opinions probably don't align perfectly with how God views you. However, there is a way to reconcile them. You can live a life in which others love you and appreciate your qualities, all while being blessed by the grace and goodness of God that emanates from you, enriching other people's lives as well.

To explore this idea, let's start with the following scripture:

> *And Mary said: "My soul magnifies the Lord, and my spirit has rejoiced in God my Savior."*
>
> **—Luke 1:46–47**

In these verses, pay attention to the words *soul* and *spirit*. When we think of possessing our souls, we may be misled into believing that our personalities are ours to dictate or that we have the right to determine how they operate.

Look more closely at what Mary said: "My soul magnifies the Lord, and my spirit has rejoiced in God my Savior" (Luke 1:46–47). What was leading the way in Mary's life? The indwelling Spirit.

Intriguingly, when Mary said that, she couldn't have fully understood what she was saying, because the Holy Spirit hadn't yet been fully revealed. However, she made the choice to walk with God, to love God, and to trust Him. Her spirit had already given thanks, so when she received a message from an angel, she was able to reply as she did.

The Spirit was leading the way in Mary's life, and He can lead the way in your life. That's how we experience the abundance God is offering us.

> *Beloved, I pray that you may prosper in all things and be in health, just as your soul prospers.*
> *—3 John 1:2*

How does the soul prosper? By letting the Spirit lead!

A few years ago, I heard about a pastor who found out that his wife had committed adultery. As soon as I heard that story, I thought of a family member who once left his wife and children and had an adulterous affair, later marrying his mistress. Many years later, he talked to me about it. He said, "The thrill was really something. But the consequences, heartache, and damage I caused—I wish I had never done it."

Now, how do you think the pastor reacted to learning that his wife had committed adultery? He didn't respond in the Spirit. Instead, he went out and committed adultery himself. Discovering his wife's infidelity must have been incredibly hurtful, but the Spirit would not have led the pastor to respond in that way. The wrong part of his being was in the

THE REAL YOU FULLY ALIVE

driver's seat.

It's said that hurt people hurt people, but these stories reveal something deeper. They show that when our spirits, which should be aligned with God, aren't in control, the damaged parts of our souls will take the lead.

Remember that the spiritual battle is taking place in your soul. It's in your mind, will, and emotions. The enemy was after these people. Their souls weren't healthy, and their families and loved ones were caught up in the mess that followed.

It's not my intention to make you feel condemned by pointing out healthy versus unhealthy souls. If you've fallen, no matter what sin you've committed, there is peace in Jesus' name. I don't stand as someone who condemns you; I am no one's judge. While I haven't committed adultery, my life is far from perfect. The Bible says that even lusting after another is committing adultery in your heart, so I will never stand in judgment of someone else.

I am here to tell you that if you have sinned or your soul is unhealthy, you can be made well. You can be healed. You don't have to live in a place of doubt and shame any longer.

If you're the one who was hurt or betrayed, you, too, can be healed. Grace, blessing, and abundance can still come into your life.

If you're reading this and entertaining the idea of an affair or any other intentional sin, listen to me. I have one word to say to you: *don't*. It won't do for you what you think it's going to do. It won't bring abundance into your life. It's a temporary thrill that will ultimately bring destruction.

Sin destroys the person committing it, the other people

involved in it, and their families. Sin has a price, and it's always higher than the price the enemy quotes. It may seem like the devil takes only an inch, but soon you're so many miles down the road that you can't even see the on-ramp.

Friend, you are not meant to live in the realm of the soul, but as a child of God, connected to the eternal Spirit of God. You are a spiritual being. You possess a soul, but that doesn't mean you get to do whatever you want to do whenever you want to do it. If you want a blessed and abundant life, your soul must yield to the Spirit.

STATEMENT #3: I LIVE IN A BODY

The real you exists in your body, your temporary earth suit. Our bodies link us to the material world. They are the instruments of all our actions. What we think or emotionally feel we often do in the bodies we carry around, but our bodies shouldn't be following our souls. Our bodies should follow the Spirit.

This is crucial to understand. The real you doesn't live in the following order:

Body —> Soul —> Spirit

The real you lives in the opposite order:

Spirit —> Soul —> Body

Think of that sequence while reading the following scriptures:

> *I beseech you therefore, brethren, by the mercies of God, that you present your bodies a living sacrifice, holy, acceptable to God, which is your reasonable service.*
>
> **—Romans 12:1**

> *Or do you not know that your body is the temple of the Holy Spirit who is in you, whom you have from God, and you are not your own?*
>
> **—1 Corinthians 6:19**

Wow, those verses are moving! When I read them, I'm amazed that my broken earth suit is the temple of the Holy Spirit. I'm amazed because my body has issues, as I'm sure you have issues with your body. I battle nerve issues, allergies, and autoimmune disorders. You may have back pain, muscle cramps, arthritis, diabetes, or insomnia. How incredible is it that our bodies, with all their flaws, are actually temples of the Holy Spirit?

Most of us have at least one physical ailment (and some of us seem to have dozens). None of us are perfect, yet when we follow and believe the perfect book, the Bible, we are saved, healed, and blessed.

Since your body is God's temple, it shouldn't yield to your soul, and your soul shouldn't yield to your body. Both body and soul should follow your spirit. Recall what we discussed at the beginning of this chapter. God is a triune God, and He created you as a triune being. When your three parts operate in the proper order, everything works as it is designed to.

Are you starting to see who you really are, according to what the Bible teaches? That's not an easy feat in our society today. If you were at a barbecue and asked someone about himself, he'd probably tell you what he does for a living. Maybe he'd tell you about his passions or his hobbies. That's what we tell each other about ourselves, but it's not who we really are.

You are not your job. You're not your feelings. You're not even your passions or interests. So, who are you, really?

You are a dynamic spiritual being created in the image of God who possesses a personality while dwelling in a temporary earth suit, all while being sanctified and made ready to dwell with your Creator for all of eternity. That's who you are.

You are no ordinary being. You are a child of the living God, a cherished son or daughter, bought with a price that's far beyond your means to repay (1 Corinthians 6:20). God's love for you is beyond measure, and He desires nothing more than for you to become like Him. With each passing day, you are being molded and shaped by the Creator of the heavens and the earth, destined for a life of abundance and blessing that will never end.

That's who you are.

Chapter One Questions

Question: What roles do the three parts of your being—your spirit, your soul, and your body—currently play in your life? How do they function in relationship to one another?

_____

_____

_____

_____

_____

_____

_____

_____

_____

Question: What does it mean to have a Spirit-led life? How can having your spirit in the driver's seat help you to defeat the enemy's attacks?

_____

_____

_____

_____

_____

_____

_____

_____

_____

Question: What do you think other people see when they look at you and your life? How does this view of you compare to how God sees you? How might your new understanding of who you really are change the way you live your life?

_____

_____

_____

_____

_____

_____

_____

_____

_____

_____

Action: In this chapter, we explored three statements that help us to understand ourselves as triune beings: "I am a spiritual being," "I possess a soul," and "I live in a body." Write these three statements on a sticky note and place it where you will see it first thing in the morning and right before you go to bed. Say these statements aloud or to yourself at the beginning and end of each day and allow them to reshape your idea of who you really are.

Chapter One Notes

_____

_____

_____

_____

_____

_____

_____

_____

_____

_____

_____

_____

_____

_____

_____

_____

_____

_____

The Supremacy of the Spirit

In the previous chapter, we learned how God is three persons in one: Father, Son, and Holy Spirit. We also saw how we are three parts in one: spirit, soul, and body. In this chapter, we'll investigate how spirit, soul, and body should work together, with spirit leading the way, and we'll explore three primary benefits to living a Spirit-led life.

EMBRACING THE SUPREMACY OF SPIRIT

You are a spirit who possesses a soul and lives in a body. The Spirit of God made your spirit come alive in the first place, and He deserves the position of ultimate prominence in your being.

But you are not in the flesh but in the Spirit, if indeed the Spirit of God dwells in you.

—Romans 8:9

This verse reveals that our true identity is found in the Spirit who dwells within us. He is supposed to lead the way. We're meant to say to God, "Holy Spirit, lead the way in my life. You run the show. You provide direction. Help me think the right way, respond the right way, and make the right decisions. I trust in Your wisdom and guidance, knowing that Your plans for me are good. Keep me humble. Help me to serve others with love and compassion, reflecting Your character to those around me. I surrender my will to Yours, and I ask that You continue to lead me each day."

Note the reference to the word *flesh* in Romans 8:9. Your *flesh* is your soul and your body working together—typically against the spirit. When your body and emotions are leading the way, it can be difficult to resist temptations and sinful desires. You may stray from what God wants you to do. Unfortunately, many of us live our lives in the flesh. We're known as being angry and mean, or as having a sharp tongue. That's not the way we should be known.

As followers of Christ, we should be known as Christ was known. We should follow the Spirit's leading like Jesus did while He was here, in His body, in the flesh. To do this, we must put our trust in God and keep our eyes focused on Him.

As Paul explained, when we experience salvation, we receive a deposit of the Holy Spirit. We also have the opportunity to walk in the fullness of the Spirit and receive baptism in the Spirit.

If you honestly think, *I do not know God, and God does not know me,* that means you are not His. If you believe, *I have not had my sins forgiven, and I am not going to be with God in*

His heaven forever, then you are not His. This means the Spirit of God is not dwelling in you, and it will be impossible for you to walk in the kind of abundance He has for you.

However, the moment you ask Jesus to come into and take over your life and to forgive all your sins, you become His. That's when you become a child of God, a member of His family. You become a Christ follower. You are in league with and in line with the Holy Spirit, and you receive a deposit of that Holy Spirit. Jesus becomes your Savior.

Then, as a child of God, you have access to His kingdom and His plans for your life. As you grow in your relationship with Him, you become more like Him. You start to experience the freedom, love, joy, and peace that only He can provide. Additionally, you have the power to overcome temptation, to resist sin, and to be a light to the world. Truly, there is nothing more fulfilling than following Jesus.

Every single person has sinned. Some may do better than others, but we all have missed the mark. As the Bible says, everyone has fallen short (Romans 3:23). That's exactly why we need a Savior.

Jesus is the only one who conquered sin, death, and the grave. He is the only one who can rescue us. Deep down, we know that even our best efforts to be good aren't enough for the job. Jesus Christ is that Savior, guiding and leading us on the right path with complete understanding and unconditional love. He saves us from our own mistakes and gives us a fresh start. He is the perfect source of salvation, grace, and mercy.

When you trust Christ and ask Him to save you from the

consequences of your sin, your name is sealed and made permanent in the Lamb's book of life in heaven (Revelation
20:15). The very moment you receive Him as your Savior,
you become His.

From that point, a transformation begins. Jesus changes
your heart, renews your mind (Romans 12:2), and reshapes
your perspective on the world. Things that once mattered a
lot may not matter as much anymore, and things that were
once insignificant become very valuable. You start to live for
Christ and aim to please Him in all that you do.

Choosing Jesus every day allows Him to guide us to a life
of true fulfillment and purpose. May we always choose to follow His ways and His will for us.

The Apostle Paul taught that when we receive Jesus
Christ as our Savior, we also receive a deposit of the Holy
Spirit. However, some Christians miss the opportunity to
embrace the Holy Spirit fully, which is crucial for living a
Spirit-filled life. Setting the Holy Spirit on the backburner by
considering Him a lesser element of God takes away the
abundance that salvation brings.

Jesus wants you to be filled with the Holy Spirit, just as
He was:

*Then Jesus, being filled with the Holy Spirit, returned from
the Jordan and was led by the Spirit into the wilderness....*

—Luke 4:1

Embracing this complete fulfillment of salvation enriches
your Christian journey while on earth and empowers you to

live a Spirit-filled life. This is what happens when you fully allow Christ to be your Lord.

Simply put, it means you've chosen to say, "Lord, not my will, but Your will be done. Not life my way, according to self, but Your way, according to the Spirit" (Luke 22:42).

The Holy Spirit is God, and He is good. It's a blessing to know Him and to walk with Him. I encourage you to live that way, just as Jesus did. All four gospels teach this truth, John the Baptist spoke about it, and even the book of Acts starts with it:

...He was taken up, after He through the Holy Spirit had given commandments to the apostles whom He had chosen...

—Acts 1:2

What we need to do is straightforward—we must simply yield to the power of the Spirit of God and let Him be our guide, allowing Him to do whatever He wants in our lives.

At the beginning of this chapter, we looked at Romans 8:9. Now let's consider the next verse:

And if Christ is in you, the body is dead because of sin, but the Spirit is life because of righteousness.

—Romans 8:10

Did you notice the *if* at the beginning of that verse? In the previous chapter, I mentioned how that particular English word doesn't exactly capture the original meaning of the Greek word. The word *if* in the Bible doesn't always indicate a condition. Consider this playful sentence: *If Lionel had millions of dollars, he would buy a vacation home.* The condition is that Lionel must have the money before he can buy the home, right? Yet, when we see Greek translated into English, the word *if* often means *since*, which can make a sentence not conditional at all.[5] Thus, *since* Lionel has a million dollars, he *can* buy said home.

So, when we read the words "if Christ is in you" in Romans 8:10, we know that it means "since Christ is in you." Note the similar case in the next verse of Romans:

> But if the Spirit of Him who raised Jesus from the dead dwells in you, He who raised Christ from the dead will also give life to your mortal bodies through His Spirit who dwells in you.
>
> **—Romans 8:11**

I love that verse. It's about the Spirit of God leading the way in our lives. It's about us living like we are spiritual beings, not merely emotional, fleshly beings who live according to our whims and urges. We are meant to live according to the abundant blessing of life that the Spirit of God has put within us.

To access this abundant life, all we have to do is pray a single sentence, such as: "Lord, take control of all aspects of my life." But we don't have to stop there. We can add, "I want to live a life that reflects Your love, grace, and mercy. Help me to walk in Your ways and follow Your commands. Teach me to love others as You have loved me. I want to be a light in this dark world, leading others to You. Strengthen my faith so I may trust in You with all my heart. May Your Spirit guide me toward the abundant life that You have planned for me. I choose now to receive Your Holy Spirit."

There are three main benefits to acknowledging the supremacy of the Holy Spirit and choosing to live a Spirit-led life. First, you receive life, not death. Second, you become part of a spiritual family. And third, you get help in your communication with God.

BENEFIT #1: YOU RECEIVE LIFE, NOT DEATH

> *There is therefore now no condemnation to those who are in Christ Jesus, who do not walk according to the flesh, but according to the Spirit. For the law of the Spirit of life in Christ Jesus has made me free from the law of sin and death.*
>
> **—Romans 8:1-2**

See the words "the law of the Spirit of life"? That's one of the four names given to the Holy Spirit in chapter 8 of Romans:

- the Spirit of life (Romans 8:2, 10)
- the Spirit of Christ (Romans 8:9)
- the Spirit of God (Romans 8:9, 14)
- the Spirit of adoption (Romans 8:15).

These are four aspects of the Holy Spirit that we can receive and embody, helping us live a blessed and abundant life.

33

Now I'd like to shine a spotlight on the beginning of Romans 8:1: "There is therefore now no condemnation to those who are in Christ Jesus." There is no condemnation. None. No death. No bondage. No more, *The devil made me do it.* No more, *I can't help it.* No more, *I was born this way.* In Christ Jesus, there is freedom from all of that. There is hope, there is salvation, and there is no longer any condemnation. It's amazing what Jesus has done for us! He has provided a way for us to be set free from sin and death.

You don't have to sin anymore. You're not chained to sin any longer. You've been set free by the grace of a loving God. He deposited His Spirit within you so that you could understand the difference between condemnation and conviction (John 16:13–15; 2 Corinthians 1:22).

We must understand that there should be no condemnation existing in our minds or coming from the depths of our being. Why? Because we're God's children and He does not condemn us. He convicts us, but He does not condemn us.

The devil condemns. The devil tells us, "You messed up. You're hopeless. You're worthless. You're no good."

That's not God. So, how does God operate? He tells us, "Come on up here. I want to help you."

God shows us the wrong in what we've done, but He also gives us the way to repentance, forgiveness, and growth. That's conviction. God loves us, even when we mess up, and doesn't want us to be weighed down by condemnation. God always draws us to Himself (John 6:44). The Holy Spirit draws us to God and convicts us of sin.

If you still feel condemnation, then the enemy has

illegitimate access to your life. You do not have to allow him to condemn you. Why? Because he cannot condemn you before God. You have not received death. You have received the Spirit of life, and you can live through Him.

I have come that they may have life, and that they may have it more abundantly.

—John 10:10

That's how Jesus put it. It's what He wants for us. That's why He came!

Abundant life is about quality of life. It's about living close to God. It's a life that is virtually free from stress, grief, worry, and fear. You can enjoy every day and look forward to more. You can sense God's nearness, and you have His help with your thoughts and actions. It's a thriving existence full of the knowledge that, regardless of how bad things seem on this earth, everything works for your good.

Have you seen the movie *Braveheart*?[6] It's a gory film, but wow, it sure has a memorable scene! I'm talking about the scene in which William Wallace, played by Mel Gibson, rallies his army of Scottish misfits to fight against the tyranny of English rule. He yells, "What will you do without freedom?"

I have a similar question: how would it be to live a life in God *without* freedom?

Bondage is not what God has for you. He wants you to understand the power of life. That's one of the benefits of letting the Holy Spirit be in charge within you: you receive life, not death. You receive encouragement, not discouragement. You receive conviction, which always helps you, not condemnation, which always hinders you.

The power of life is within your grasp. Allow the Holy Spirit to guide your steps, and feel the transforming energy that comes with it. Let go of discouragement and grab hold of long-lasting peace and meaningful purpose today.

BENEFIT #2: YOU BECOME PART OF A SPIRITUAL FAMILY

When you live a Spirit-led life, you become part of a spiritual family. In this family, there's no need for competition or comparison, because the Spirit provides each person with unique gifts and talents. Everyone is valued and loved just for being part of the family. There are sometimes challenges and disagreements, but love and unity in the family prevail.

The moment you ask Jesus Christ to come in, take over, and forgive your sins, a deposit of the Holy Spirit is made, and the fullness of God can come into your life. When that transaction happens, you receive life and enter the family of God. If you let Jesus place you fully into His Spirit, you will start living a Spirit-filled life.

For as many as are led by the Spirit of God, these are sons of God. For you did not receive the spirit of bondage again to fear, but you received the Spirit of adoption by whom we cry out, "Abba, Father."

—Romans 8:14–15

You are spirit, soul, and body. Which one is going to lead the way in your life? I propose that we all let the Spirit lead the way because He is God, He is good, and He loves us more than we love ourselves.

We read in Romans 8:14 that we are "led by the Spirit," but what does that mean? Well, there are several ways we can picture being *led*.

One way to be led is to be tugged or pulled along. This is how many of us are led by the Spirit. Even when we disagree with Him and think we know better, He still leads us along for our own good. This creates unnecessary struggles and problems in our lives.

Once, when my wife and I were grocery shopping, we saw a little kid pitching a fit in the produce section. While he was kicking and screaming, he was simultaneously watching cartoons on his mother's phone! My wife and I couldn't believe the multitasking skills of this young boy.

Horrified yet fascinated, we watched the mother literally drag her son along the floor as she continued shopping. She dragged him to the apples, let go of his hand, and he continued his temper tantrum and cartoon watching. She put apples in her cart, dragged him along the floor to the peppers, dropped his hand, and put peppers in her cart. If multitasking were an Olympic event, this lady would win gold every time!

Watching them, my wife and I were entertained and astonished at the same time. We also felt sorry for them. It struck me that many Christians have a similar relationship with the Holy Spirit. He has given us everything we need. He blesses us, yet we resist Him to the point that He has to drag us along.

Besides being pulled and dragged, another way to be *led* by the Spirit is like when a father places his hand on the head of a walking child and gently guides her away from trouble.

Sometimes, being *led* looks like a mother picking up her child and simply holding him. This reminds me of how the Spirit adopts us and helps us as children of God. He may pick us up and hold us until we're ready to listen and let Him lead. This is an approach I sometimes took with my sons. Instead of disciplining them, I held them tightly until they chilled out and quit fussing.

Sometimes, being *led* means actually being carried to where we need to go. There were moments when my children were too tired to keep going, so I'd pick them up and place them on my shoulders.

Since we are led by the Spirit, and since we are children of God, how about we just reach up and take the hand of the Spirit? How about we simply surrender and enjoy walking with God wherever He leads us? To be part of the family of God means to accept our position as His child. This automatically means that He should have the authority to take our hand and lead us. He knows the best way, and we can't see past our fingertips. That way is a lot better than pitching a fit and yelling, "That's not what I want! I want it my way!"

Everyone can be led by the Spirit. It's not complicated. You simply tune into His frequency and tune out the enemy's frequency.

The idea of tuning out or into the Spirit reminds me of a

well-known cautionary tale about a careless park ranger. At Yellowstone National Park, a ranger was leading a group of hikers to a scenic overlook near a ranger fire-observation station. He was so intent on educating the hikers on the flowers and animals that he became annoyed by the messages on his two-way radio, so he switched it off. As the group neared the tower, the ranger was met by a breathless lookout, who said, "Why did you turn your radio off? We've been trying to warn you that a grizzly bear has been seen following your party!"

Turn your radio on and tune into the Spirit! Anytime we tune out the Holy Spirit or ignore warnings from God in the Bible, we put ourselves and those around us in danger.

Don't let outside distractions or overwhelming emotions take your focus away from the Spirit's guidance. Pay attention to the red flags and convictions you feel when you step outside of God's will. His Word is a guide, protector, and light that keeps us on the right path (Psalm 119:105). We shouldn't ignore the warnings it gives us.

There are predators of wickedness and evil stalking you, just waiting to pounce on and destroy you. But I've got good news. God loves you more than the enemy hates you, and He certainly has a better plan for you than what your enemy has in store. God wants to help you. The question is: will you yield to Him and receive His help?

Part of being in God's family is reaping all the benefits of being connected to life-giving sources. You receive salvation, the leading of the Holy Spirit, and a deep sense of belonging. You're connected. You're tuned in. You're part of a community that shares the same values, hopes, and dreams as you.

You can find comfort in knowing that you're never alone and there are people who are always there for you, supporting you in the good times as well as the tough times. The best part? You get to experience the love of a Father who will never abandon you—who will always guide you in the right direction.

When I teach, I feel so humbled seeing the congregation sitting in rows in front of me. At church, the reason we sit in rows is that we want to accommodate as many people as possible to be taught the Word of God. I try my best to make my message engaging and relevant, something that resonates with each person in the crowd. It's important to me that they leave with a sense of inspiration and guidance. Every time I see people leaving with smiles on their faces or stopping to shake my hand and thank me for the message, I know that I'm doing something right. At the end of the day, it's all about helping others and sharing the love and teachings of Jesus.

Rows are great, but there comes a time when you need to sit in a circle as well. That's why, every week, I encourage churchgoers to join a small group, so they can connect with others in a more intimate way.

In a massive group of people, there's no way to get to know everyone. But in a small group, you certainly can. You can pray for them, and they can pray for you. Those connections can really be strong when you're sitting in a circle. There is nothing like having a spiritual family to walk through life with.

BENEFIT #3: YOU GET HELP IN YOUR COMMUNICATION WITH GOD

Another benefit of living a Spirit-led life is that your communication with God gets a boost.

> *Likewise the Spirit also helps in our weaknesses. For we do not know what we should pray for as we ought, but the Spirit Himself makes intercession for us with groanings which cannot be uttered.*
>
> **—Romans 8:26**

Many people think that this reference to *groanings* is related to speaking in tongues. However, this is not referring to tongues. It's not prayer language. Instead, this reference means "prayers that do not have utterance."[7]

So, the Holy Spirit is praying within you, and it's not an utterance. It's a spirit-sound, not a human sound.

If you've trusted Christ and asked Him to come in and forgive your sins, then the Spirit of God is within you right now, praying for you. He is lifting up a sound to the throne room of God in the third heaven—a sound that can't be understood by angels, demons, or anyone else. It goes all the way up, and it's a sound only the Spirit can make.

Let's read the following verse in Romans, noting that the word *hearts* refers to the soul:

> *Now He who searches the hearts knows what the mind of the Spirit is, because He makes intercession for the saints according to the will of God.*
>
> **—Romans 8:27**

41

So, will we allow that to happen—for Him to search us and pray for us? We just have to say, "Lord, I'm not afraid. I'm not going to run away from anything You have for me. I want it all—Your blessings in my mind, my prayers, and my body. Lord, I choose to follow You and live for You."

When you make that choice, and let the Spirit of God who dwells within you lead the way in your mind and body, life becomes more blessed than you've ever experienced. It becomes awesome—phenomenal! Why? Because there's communication between you and God going on all the time.

This reminds me of one of my favorite jokes about prayer. A family invited some friends over for dinner. At the dinner table, the mother asked their six-year-old daughter to say the prayer before the meal.

"Mommy, I don't know what to say," the young girl replied.

"Just say what you heard me say earlier today," the mother said.

The little girl bowed her head and prayed, "Dear Lord, why on earth did I invite all these people over here to dinner?"

I share this anecdote for two reasons. One, it's hilarious. Two, unfortunately, many of us don't know how to pray. We don't know how to connect with God.

It's not that hard; you just make a choice to step into it. Once you do, it becomes an integral part of your faith walk.

If you haven't prayed before, here are a few suggestions.

- Find a quiet place to pray.

- Begin with praise and thanksgiving.

- Confess your sins.

- Ask for forgiveness, guidance, and wisdom.

- Pray for others.

- Close by saying, "In Jesus' name, amen."

Praying this way doesn't have to be long, drawn out, or complicated. It's simply having a conversation with someone who already knows you better than you know yourself. Praying gives you a direct connection to the God of creation, who created *you*. It's a crucial step in moving toward the path of complete abundance.

An abundant, Spirit-led life isn't free of challenges, but it can be simple—as simple as choosing to receive life over death. As you let the Spirit lead the way, you'll also be blessed as part of a spiritual family. Plus, having a conversation with your heavenly Father will, in fact, become that much easier.

Chapter Two Questions

Question: Is the Holy Spirit currently convicting you of anything? What is the difference between conviction and condemnation? Do you still feel condemned, or are you living fully in the freedom Jesus provides for you to repent, receive God's forgiveness, and grow?

_____

_____

_____

_____

_____

_____

_____

_____

_____

_____

_____

Question: In what ways are you engaging with the family of believers? Do love and unity prevail in your relationships with other Christians, or do you tend to get caught up in comparison and competition? In what ways will you begin or continue providing comfort, encouragement, and support to your brothers and sisters in Christ?

_____

_____

_____

_____

_____

_____

_____

_____

_____

_____

Question: How is your prayer life? Do you pray throughout the day, once a day, or only in church on Sundays? How will you begin following the Holy Spirit's lead in your communication with God?

_____

_____

_____

_____

_____

_____

_____

_____

_____

_____

Action: Consider how you respond to the leading of the Holy Spirit. Do you argue with Him and put up a fuss when you don't agree with His guidance and warnings? Do you ignore Him? What happens in your life when you respond in these ways? Take a moment to imagine what your life might look like if you were to take God's hand and walk with Him, allowing Him to lead you according to His ways and His plans and make you more like Jesus. Are you ready and willing to step into an abundantly blessed life as God's child?

_____

_____

_____

_____

_____

_____

_____

_____

_____

_____

Chapter Two Notes

Winning the Battle in Your Mind

You are created in the image of God (Genesis 1:27), who is in three persons: Father, Son, and Holy Spirit. You are also composed of three parts: spirit, soul, and body. The soul, in turn, consists of three elements: mind, will, and emotions. This is essential to remember because everything starts with a thought, right in the seat of your soul. Spiritual battles begin with a thought, and our souls are the battlefield.

If you belong to Christ, the throne of His grace has the highest seat in your soul. All too often, however, a thought leads us to an emotional response that isn't good. It causes harm to us and to the person we're responding emotionally against. It's only natural to focus on our emotions, thoughts, and body, regardless of whether they're healthy or unhealthy, but there's so much more to us than that.

Let's dig into how we can live abundantly in our mind and win the battles that rage against this area of our soul.

MIND GAMES: THE UNTOLD SPIRITUAL BATTLE

Have you ever experienced a battle in your mind? Have you ever had thoughts come in that you instantly disliked and wondered where they came from? They come unbidden, revealing aspects of yourself that you disagree with and don't fully understand.

Well, there are ways to win the battles in your mind. Before any other way, we must first turn to the Word of God, because there's nothing like it that can guide our lives when we store it in our hearts. It show us how to let the Spirit lead us to victory.

In Romans, we see the first passage that gives us clear instruction about how we can win the battle of the mind by allowing the Spirit to lead our soul—our mind, will, and emotions:

> For those who live according to the flesh set their minds on the things of the flesh, but those who live according to the Spirit, the things of the Spirit. For to be carnally minded is death, but to be spiritually minded is life and peace.
>
> **—Romans 8:5–6**

When you read that passage, remember that the word *flesh* is a reference to your body, particularly those parts of your body that want to be satisfied, including your stomach, hormones, and so on. The flesh works in partnership with the soul to wrest control from the spirit.

So, don't live according to the flesh. In other words, don't live according to your whims, desires, and impulses. Instead, live according to the Spirit, as the Word of God instructs you to do.

It's scary to think of spiritual warfare happening in our minds, but it's true. Your part in the kingdom battle is happening in that space between your ears.

How is it happening? Your flesh is battling against your spirit. The things of the world are in conflict with the real you, which is your spirit. The things of the carnal mind—the things of this realm—are in opposition to what you should be thinking about to live the blessed life that Jesus wants you to live.

Let's read the last part of that verse again:

> *For to be carnally minded is death, but to be spiritually minded is life and peace.*
>
> **—Romans 8:6**

People who are "carnally minded" are so focused on the here and now that they downgrade God to an afterthought.

It's exciting to know that the direct result of being "spiritually minded" is having life and peace. I believe we all want that. To have life means that you're willing to step into the highest and best that God gives. God is spirit and light. He is the giver of life, and He *is* life.

In Romans 8:6, *life* refers to what we can receive from God, which is much better than what we can give ourselves. *Peace* is a reference to health, harmony, and prosperity. God's peace calms the storm that rages in our minds. He wants the turmoil to stop.

When turbulent thoughts pop into my mind, I stop to consider their source. I know they didn't come from God, so they must have come either from worldly influences or from the enemy.

Sometimes I feel powerless in the battle within my own mind. Maybe you feel the same way. I'm frequently asking the Lord, *How do I set my mind? What can I do to make sure I'm heavenly-minded?* The real pickle is that if we can't be heavenly-minded, then we can't be the "earthly good" God wants to help us be.

SETTING YOUR MIND

To understand the importance of where you set your mind, consider the following passage:

If then you were raised with Christ, seek those things which are above, where Christ is, sitting at the right hand of God. Set your mind on things above, not on things on the earth.

—Colossians 3:1–2

Reading these verses, we can see that the concept of meditation came from God. That's right. The world stole meditation, made it weird, and corrupted it. Meditation is not all of that "New Age" stuff you hear about on TV or in movies. It's simply being aware of how to put your thoughts on where God is. It's focusing on the Lord.

When you meditate, you clear your mind and focus on

God. You allow yourself to be in His presence and open yourself up to His guidance. It's a powerful practice that can bring clarity, peace, and direction to your life.

Meditation means investing time with God, keeping your mind on where He is, knowing that He will help you do better in this life and prevent you from messing it up by doing things your way.

In the above passage, we can again replace *if* with *since*. "If then you were raised with Christ" should be interpreted "since you were raised with Christ." These verses address people who have already asked Jesus Christ to come into their lives and forgive their sins—people who have said, "I'm not going to live my way any longer. I want to live my life Your way." The very moment you do that, you are saved and are raised with Christ. Your trajectory in life changes infinitely for the better.

Think about it. Deep inside, you know that your best efforts to be good enough won't cut it. That's why you need a Savior. When you trust in Christ and receive the forgiveness of sins only He can offer, you are, spiritually speaking, raised up. In that very moment, your eternal address changes from *down below* to *up above*, with God.

Perhaps the most important part of this passage is Paul's encouragement in verse 2: "Set your mind on things above, not on things on the earth."

Here's a simple technique about meditation (the God-focused kind) that I learned from a man named Gene Edwards at a men's retreat many years ago. His lesson was all about helping us choose where our minds go. At the time, I didn't even know that choice was possible.

A tall man with white hair and a white beard, Edwards showed me how we can be lifted during worship or prayer into the throne room. The throne in heaven is mentioned in Isaiah 6, Revelation 4, and Revelation 19. In those three passages, we see a picture of the place God Himself actually is right now, and that's where we can go in our minds.

Edwards brought a beautiful image to my attention. He said that the Bible describes God as sitting on a throne (Isaiah 6:1) and that He lights up all of heaven (Revelation 21:23). This light is so powerful that it could have downright bleached Jesus' robe, turning it completely white. The train of His robe—which signifies His authority and His right to rule—fills the whole temple in heaven (Isaiah 6:1). That same light from God's presence, Edwards suggested, would be so brilliant that it could've bleached Jesus' hair and beard as well! This humorous but beautiful picture can draw us further into God's utmost holiness and the holiness of Christ's intercession for us—something very much worth meditating on.

Over the years, each time I've meditated on those descriptions and images, they've moved me. Edwards also spoke of heavenly beings worshipping God without ceasing. They cry, "Holy, holy, holy is the LORD of hosts; the whole earth is full of His glory!" (Isaiah 6:3).

He taught that there is something in heaven that resembles "a sea of glass" (Revelation 4:6) and that people from every tribe, tongue, and nation in the history of creation will be there worshipping God (Revelation 7:9). Wow, that got me excited!

At one point on this men's retreat, Edwards called the twenty or so of us forward and asked us to form a huddle. When we did, I thought, *This is weird, and it's about to get weirder*, but we trusted him. We understood that, because Edwards was a teacher, he was committed to helping us see deeper truths so that we could live an abundant life as Christian men.

We all gathered close together. He said, "Closer, closer." We jammed in together, and as he lifted his hands, he began to sing: "I love You, Lord. And I lift my voice to worship You. Oh, my soul, rejoice."[8]

Being so close, we heard each other sing and sensed that we were entering into the presence of God together. I kept my eyes closed because I thought if I opened them, I'd be literally blinded by the glory of God. That's how powerful this moment was.

Isn't it interesting that my emotions had incorrectly predicted that this experience would be strange and uncomfortable? Far from being weird, it was a practice found in the Bible and should be a part of all of our lives!

At that men's retreat, after ditching my feelings that this was weird and going to get weirder, I made the choice to enter in. I've never been the same.

Since then, every time I close my eyes when I'm worshipping, I go to that place, into the presence of the Lord. When I pray, I often follow the example of numerous people described in the Bible as kneeling down, humbling themselves in the glory of the Creator of the heavens and the earth.

My experience at the men's retreat is just one illustration of the benefits that result from setting your mind on the place where real life exists—where the three persons of the Godhead dwell together in great glory.

When we choose to be earthly good and not earthly-minded, everything changes for the better. Living our lives with the Lord—allowing our thoughts and actions to be motivated and directed by the grace and goodness of God—leads to lasting, positive transformations. Setting our minds on the Lord doesn't make us weird; it just helps us tune in to the right frequency.

For me, it keeps me in a place of trust. When I choose to worship and pray, and when I read God's words, sometimes I close my eyes and start giving thanks.

Thank You, Lord, for life, health, peace, and healing. Thank You for my marriage, for my family, and for Your prayers right now. Thank You for Your abundant grace and for establishing my steps, as Your Word says in Psalm 40:2. I know that in You, and only You, I am righteous. Thank You, Lord.

When I express gratitude like that, my mindset changes, as does my awareness of God's nearness. I urge you to grab hold of His truth. Doing so will change what happens in your mind. Connecting with the Lord doesn't take much time or effort. When you do, your trust in Him and quality of life will increase.

If you have any doubts or questions, I want to encourage you to continue reading and searching for answers. In the end, you will find that God's love for you is real, and once you truly understand and accept that love, your life will change in amazing ways.

Remember that God is always near and His love is always available. To explore these truths, I'll share an inspiring anecdote that contrasts faith with doubt.

WHO WOULD LIKE TO FLY A KITE?

A young girl was flying a kite on a windy day, the kite going higher and higher. Finally, it went so high that she couldn't see it anymore.

A man walked up and saw the girl holding a reel with string coiled around it. The man saw the taut string coming out of the reel, reaching up into the clouds. High above him, even though he couldn't see the kite, he could hear sharp, cracking sounds—the kite flapping in the breeze.

The man asked, "How do you even know you have a kite up there?"

The girl thought for a moment of the vast trove of evidence proving the kite's existence. Instead, she simply replied, "Because I can feel it."

That's the way it is when you're used to the presence of the Lord. Although we can't see the Holy Spirit, we can sense His work in our lives. We can sense His presence and that He is changing us into the image of Christ.

Remember that you determine what resides in your mind. If your thoughts revolve around the here and now, fixated on your whims, and if your flesh is working against the Spirit, then you'll be in a constant, never-ending mental battle.

On the other hand, if you choose to set your mind on the Lord, you'll be letting God's Spirit work powerfully in you. You'll experience transformation, and you'll be able to discern truth from lies.

So, choose wisely what you allow to reside in your mind. Fill your mind with things that honor God and aid your spiritual growth. When you do these things, you'll experience a peace that passes understanding (Philippians 4:7), and you'll be able to take every thought captive to obey Christ (2 Corinthians 10:5).

Remember that your mind is a powerful weapon that can work either for you or against you. You must cultivate the discipline of guarding your thoughts and filling your mind with truth.

It's doable. You just have to take a time-out from all the craziness in your world. Take a break from the spin. Defend yourself against the negativity being shot at you. It makes a difference—a huge difference.

There are many ways you can focus less on the devil and more on God. You can renew your mind daily by reading His Word. You can strengthen your relationship with Him by seeking His guidance. You can seek fellowship with like-minded believers, who will help you stay tuned into His frequency. You can focus on the light that God brings in dark times and trust in His love and grace. Those are just some quick tips. In the next few sections, we're going to dive deep into three practical ways you can win the battle of your mind.

Practical Step #1: Identify Where the Enemy Is Infiltrating Your Mind

First things first, we must identify how the enemy gets into our minds and invades our thoughts. The evil one attacks through fear, insecurity, and doubt. The deceiver intrudes with unbelief, anger, and frustration. The father of lies infests through lust, greed, and jealousy.

These negative thoughts can consume us, preventing us from seeing the good in ourselves, in others, and in God. Everyone experiences these thoughts, and it's essential to remember that God is here to help us, not to condemn us.

Now, let's look at a verse that can help with resisting the enemy's attacks:

Be sober, be vigilant....

—1 Peter 5:8

While being *sober* can mean not wandering around aimlessly in a drunken stupor, here it's referring to a state of mind. It's about being sober-*minded*. In this context, the word *sober* is less about bodily wanderings and more about mental wanderings. It's about stopping the devil from tricking us into believing the negative thoughts we tell ourselves: *I can't do this. I'm not good enough. I'm such a failure. I don't deserve to be happy.*

God knows you inside and out, and He knows that with Him in your life, you can do this. You are good enough. You are a success. You can be happy.

Being *vigilant* means paying attention to and examining the thoughts coming into your mind. It's about preventing devilish notions from entering and taking root. Don't give the enemy any of your mental time or space. Scripture tells us how to do this:

> *Therefore submit to God. Resist the devil and he will flee from you.*
>
> **—James 4:7**

Choosing to worship and set our minds on God makes all the difference in the world. We shouldn't focus on the devil because he is a defeated foe. Paying attention to him just leads to thoughts of fear and anxiety, which aren't from God.

Instead, when we concentrate on God, we receive peace and a sense of security. By dwelling on His goodness and mercy, we can trust that He has a plan for our lives and that He is in control.

Ultimately, shifting our focus from the devil to God can help us to fight against temptation, live victoriously, and fulfill our God-given purpose.

These ideas are perfectly captured by a real-life incident I saw documented on social media. In an Indian village, a leopard chased a stray dog into an outdoor bathroom. The owner of the bathroom, upon hearing a crazy commotion, went outside, stood on a ladder, and looked over the walls of the bathroom stall. After seeing the leopard and dog inside, he locked the door and called the authorities.

The two animals were trapped inside for many hours. Miraculously, the dog survived, traumatized yet otherwise unharmed. A photo shows them sitting in opposite corners, the dog awake and vigilant, and the leopard—sleeping. The dog didn't take his eyes off the enemy the entire night. He didn't sleep. He didn't move. The dog just sat watching, but the leopard didn't attack him.

Why didn't the leopard kill and devour the dog? Authorities familiar with leopards in that part of India explained that they usually attack their prey from behind. That big cat, being out of his element, must have been disoriented in the small, confined area. When the authorities arrived the next morning, the leopard managed to escape.[9]

When I heard this story and saw the photo, it struck me that this is what often happens between us and the enemy. The devil gets close, and we get confused, unsure of how to resist him and submit to God. We struggle to set our minds on God because the enemy is after us.

In those moments, we face a choice. Like the dog's decision to stay alert and face his enemy, we have to decide ahead of time to stay sober-minded and never let Satan win. In this way, we block the enemy's inroads into our thoughts and replace them with roadblocks.

PRACTICAL STEP #2: BUILD—IN—A—PAUSE!

One way to stay vigilant against devilish thoughts is to pause.

When I'm hit with thoughts that I know didn't come from God, I take a moment to collect myself and think, *Wait a second. That didn't come from God. God doesn't curse. God doesn't tempt anyone, because He is not tempted by evil* (James 1:13). Then, I emotionally step back from those negative thoughts and set my mind on God, saying, "I am Yours, God. I love You with all my heart."

You can do this, too. You can take a step back from the road the enemy is trying to lead you down, and you can erect a barricade—you can win the battle of your mind.

PRACTICAL STEP #3: USE THE WORD TO FIGHT BACK

To learn how to fight back, consider the following scripture:

> Be anxious for nothing, but in everything by prayer and supplication, with thanksgiving, let your requests be made known to God; and the peace of God, which surpasses all understanding, will guard your hearts and minds through Christ Jesus.
>
> **—Philippians 4:6–7**

When reading this passage, be aware that the word *understanding* is a reference to the mind and our thoughts[10], while the word *guard* can be thought of like an umpire.

I understand that there are times when anxiety strikes. I'm curious, have you wondered whether Jesus was ever anxious?

He didn't seem anxious when, as a twelve-year-old boy,

WINNING THE BATTLE IN YOUR MIND

He upset His parents by staying in the temple too long (Luke 2:41–52). He didn't seem apprehensive when John the Baptist baptized Him (Luke 3:21–22). He didn't even seem to be worried when the Spirit of God led Him into the wilderness to be tempted by the devil (Matthew 4; Luke 4).

He fasted for forty days. Can you imagine the immense willpower and mental control needed to go without food for forty days? Forty days! His stomach certainly wasn't leading the way. His Spirit was.

I'm not bragging, but I once fasted—drinking only water—for six days. On the sixth day, while playing with our kids on the floor, I became so weak that I couldn't get up. I asked my wife, Dawn, to bring me some pineapple juice. Two minutes after drinking it, I felt the sugar flowing through me so fast that I thought I was getting high. But I digress.

If I was that feeble after less than a week of fasting—and if you've fasted, you know what it's like to feel so frail—can you imagine how Jesus was feeling? Try to picture yourself in His position—having fasted for forty days and then being tempted by the devil with a rock that looked like a loaf of bread.

Now when the tempter came to Him, he said, "If You are the Son of God, command that these stones become bread."
—Matthew 4:3

How did Jesus respond?

63

But He answered and said, "It is written, 'Man shall not live by bread alone, but by every word that proceeds from the mouth of God.'"

—Matthew 4:4

Jesus' response proves that during potentially the most anxious moment up to that point in His life—when He was getting hit hard with temptation—He was able to push the enemy away with the Word of God stored in His heart.

If you're connecting with God's Word, it will also work for you. Find scriptures that help you in the areas where you struggle most. Remember that the things you think about determine the quality of your life.

When I get hit with fear, self-doubt, or paranoia, I tell myself, *God didn't give me the spirit of fear. God didn't give me the spirit of self-doubt. God didn't give me the spirit of paranoia. God gave me love, power, and a sound mind* (2 Timothy 1:7). Boom! My fear, self-doubt, and paranoia vanish.

An effective way to use the Word of God against our enemy is to memorize Scripture. Why is this crucial? Because when God's Word is in our minds, the battles of the enemy and our flesh are diminished. The Lord will extinguish those fires in our thoughts.

An example from my own life occurred when I was out in my garden, cutting weeds with a machete. I was chopping vines that, if left alone, would wrap around my trees and slowly kill them. So, I was using the machete to hack at the vines at the base of the trees.

Suddenly, I saw one of my neighbors running straight

toward me, waving his arms and yelling, "Leave those trees alone! Those trees don't deserve what you're doing to them!" Knowing from prior experience that this man had some mental health issues, I figured that reasoning with him probably wouldn't achieve much. So, all I said was, "I'm actually helping these trees." That didn't stop him—he just kept yelling at me.

For a split second, I wanted to give him a piece of my mind. I even fantasized about pointing the machete at him to get his attention. Yet, I quickly decided *not* to give in to those emotions. Instead, I thought of the following verse:

> *Go from the presence of a foolish man, when you do not perceive in him the lips of knowledge.*
>
> **—Proverbs 14:7**

I decided just to walk away from him, and that was that. Crisis—and sin—averted, partly thanks to my ability to remember Scripture in the heat of the moment.

If memorizing Scripture isn't a regular practice for you, I'd like to ask a couple of questions. Do you feel a strong connection or natural attraction to the Bible? If not, what do you think is preventing your connection to God's Word?

Scripture gives us life every day. It renews our souls. It restores our minds. It is our daily bread. By revealing to us *who* we really are and *whose* we are, Scripture shows us what real life is all about. When we are focused on and being fed by God and His Word, we can quickly recall truths that help us fight the enemy.

A simple technique to help you memorize God's Word is to add scriptures to your screensaver. The screensaver was invented decades ago, and I like to think that for the past thirty or so years, Christians around the world have been seeing Scripture on their screensavers every day. Imagine how much of the Bible they must have memorized by now!

You can also write scriptures on sticky notes and post them around the house: on the inside of kitchen cupboards, on your bathroom mirror, or beside the button that opens your garage door. Be sure to change it up. Every week or so, pick completely new places to post your sticky notes.

Since our spiritual battles start in the mind, we must know where the enemy slips in. Recognize the areas of your life where thoughts tend to be open for attack. Is it greediness, lust, anger, doubt? Know the inlets that Satan uses to infiltrate your mind and decisions.

When thoughts pop in, practice "the pause." Practicing "the pause" means to simply take a moment to check those thoughts against the truth of God's Word and see if they are from God or from the enemy. If you know your adversary is shooting arrows into your mind, then use those memorized scriptures to fight back—hard!

My desire is that every spiritual battle will be an easy win for you. We already fight *from* victory because of Christ. When we take control of our minds, we make the enemy's attacks weak and futile. I want you to win those battles because I love you. From the depths of my being, I really do. I want to help you live an abundant life—a blessed life.

It all depends on letting God have control of your mind,

which controls your words, which, in turn, controls your decisions and actions. You have the power to decide. What you think is what you will do. So, who is in charge of your mind?

Chapter Three Questions

Question: What kinds of thoughts tend to rule your mind and emotions? Do these thoughts and emotions result in godly actions or harmful ones?

_____

_____

_____

_____

_____

_____

_____

_____

_____

_____

Question: How can you begin setting your mind intentionally on the things of the Spirit?

_____

_____

_____

_____

_____

_____

_____

_____

_____

_____

Question: In this chapter, I shared an anecdote about a young girl flying a kite so high that it was no longer visible. A skeptical man asked, "How do you even know you have a kite up there?" The girl replied, "Because I can feel it." Do you feel the Holy Spirit within you? Do you feel God's nearness, His goodness, His guidance, and His peace? If not, what do you think is preventing you from feeling Him? How can you connect more deeply and fully with God?

_____

_____

_____

_____

_____

_____

_____

_____

_____

_____

_____

Action: We all know the familiar saying that "an apple a day keeps the doctor away," but did you know that a scripture a day keeps the devil away? Every time you read the Bible, you open yourself up to the ways of God and invite transformation into your life. When the enemy tries to invade your mind, you can fight back with the Word of God and win the battle. When I read the Bible, I mark it up with a pen. I've done this all my life and find it indispensable for memorizing Scripture. In my Bibles, I underline and circle words. I write notes in the margins. I add stars and exclamation points all over the pages. If you haven't marked up a Bible with a pen before and you agree that it's not blasphemous to do so, try engaging with the Word of God in this way. Search for and highlight scriptures that help you in the areas where you get hit. Memorize them to store them in your mind so you have them ready to fend off the devil's attacks.

Chapter Three Notes

Choices of the Will

In this chapter, we're going to explore that part of our soul called the will. As I write this, I pray that you understand how your will connects to your choices. What we choose—and why we choose it—is not by accident; it's by design. Unfortunately, many of us don't respond to the greatness and goodness of our God in our decisions. Instead, we make choices by responding to what the enemy brings before us or to what's happening in the here and now only.

It is our will that connects us to both our bad choices and our good ones. Have you ever made a choice that you later regretted? Of course you have! We all have. I have made so many shockingly bad choices that I deeply regret. However, I have also made good choices that have brought me to where I am today.

It's important to recognize that our will is powerful, and it can get us closer to God's plan for us or steer us away from it. We must choose wisely and stay rooted in our faith and beliefs to make the best decisions. Let us strive to make choices that align with His will and purpose.

THE UPS WATERBOY

When I was around nineteen years old and in junior college, I worked at UPS each night from 10 p.m. until 2 a.m., loading and unloading packages on semitrucks. At that time, the job was all about the speed of handling packages, and I really enjoyed working hard and fast.

Eventually, the higher-ups recognized that I was a hard worker, and they wanted to promote me to a supervisory position. I was a proud member of the Teamsters Union, however, and the promotion would require me to leave the union and become a *company man*.

Well, two of the sorters I worked with—we'll call them Ron and Fred—were spitting mad about that. They'd been slogging away much longer than I had, and they believed *they* deserved the promotion, *not* me. Over the next few weeks, to put me in my place, Ron and Fred pranked me a few times with practical jokes, just to humiliate me in front of my work buddies.

Eventually, the big day arrived, and I became (not bragging here) the youngest person ever promoted to supervisor in the history of UPS in the state of Illinois.

At the beginning of my last shift as a union member, there was a small party thrown in my honor. All the guys in suits and ties were applauding, but all the guys in boots and jeans were staring daggers at me like I was a traitor.

After my shift ended at 2:30 a.m., with the temperature in the mid-thirties, I put on my brand-new jacket and got on my brand-new motorcycle. Suddenly, from behind me, five gallons of ice-cold water were thrown all over me, some of the water even going up the tailpipe of my motorcycle. There was Ron, holding the empty bucket and giggling like the Joker in Batman. He thought he'd just done the funniest thing in the world. As you might expect, I disagreed.

Wrath instantly consumed me. I chased Ron, thinking, *I'm gonna beat you to within an inch of your life!* (That thought was sin number one. There are more sins coming!)

Blinded by rage, I chased him into the building where his truck was parked on the other side. Suddenly, I fell hard onto the cement floor. Ron and his buddy Fred had set a trap for me, and I had run—literally—straight into it. Fred had been waiting for us inside the building, and a second after I sprinted past, Fred pulled an extension cord, tripping me up. Yes, I fell down, but I got up straight away, a Hulk on a mission.

I started chasing *both* of them, thinking, *I'm gonna rip you apart.* (Another bad choice. Another sin.)

The two pranksters ran outside and jumped, Dukes of Hazzard-style, into a car. The ingenious idiots had even planned their getaway! The wheels of the car spun, gravel shot into my face, and I thought, *You boys don't know what you're in for.*

I jumped on my motorcycle and pursued them—*hunted* them—but I lost them. So, I drove around the neighborhood until I finally found their car parked on the street.

I kicked the car, ran up to the house, and kicked the front door, cussing all the while. (So much sin!)

Caught in this shameful fit of anger, I yelled something really, really stupid. I roared, "You need to know that, for the rest of your lives, you're never going to be safe!"

Nobody in the house—understandably—came out to confront me, so I rode home. After taking a shower, and with it being around 3:30 in the morning, I was about to try to sleep, but the phone rang. I picked it up quickly so it wouldn't wake anyone; otherwise, there would've been even more problems.

It was the police. An officer confirmed that, yes, he was talking to Jeff Klingenberg. Then he said, "You just threatened people's lives. You need to come back to the residence of the incident." The officer would be waiting for me there.

"Are you kidding me?" I said, flabbergasted.

"No," he said sternly, "you need to get over here, now. Or else I'm coming to get you."

"I'll be right over, officer."

I pushed my motorcycle out of the garage—starting it in there would've undoubtedly woken up my family—and glided it silently down the street. I rode back to (I'm ashamed to say this, but it's true) the scene of the crime.

At the house, there was a police car with its red and blue lights spinning. There were Ron and Fred. There was also Ron's wife, who looked as if she'd been crying for a long time, and she was still crying.

That's when Ron informed me that his wife had recently

experienced some problems that had required her to be hospitalized, and it was her first day back home. It hit me then that she, too, had heard me yell, "You're never going to be safe!"

At that time in my life, I was a follower of Christ, but I wasn't walking with the Lord. I wasn't living righteously.

I asked for forgiveness from Ron and his wife and apologized profusely. Ron's wife continued bawling her eyes out.

"What can I do?" I said over and over again. "I'm so sorry."

Long story short, we all came to an agreement, and they decided not to press charges. Still, that's not the point. It's not about whether I was legally guilty or faced charges for the crime I had obviously committed. The point is that, at that time in my life, my will was weak. It was so feeble that it was almost nonexistent.

Reflecting on those disturbing few hours of my life, I can see that my mind had terrible, disgusting thoughts. My emotions were going crazy, and my will wasn't even engaged. My mind and emotions caused me to make bad choices and to respond in disgraceful ways.

As followers of Christ and children of God, we don't have to live that way. We can make choices of the will that align with the ways of God and counteract the ways of the enemy.

PREDETERMINATIONS

To ensure that your spirit, rather than your emotions, is leading the way, you can make a *predetermination*. If your weakness is lust, for example, then you can predetermine that, the next time the enemy shoots a lust arrow at you, you're going to fight back by praying for people in your life who don't know Jesus. This would be a predetermination that you set before the arrow ever comes flying at you.

Instead of entertaining the lustful thought, falling to that temptation, and acting out with your mind and body, you can reverse the whole process. When the next attack comes, your will can make the choice to fight back immediately. In this way, you'll stay connected to the indwelling Holy Spirit and live life His way—with His blessings.

This is exactly the right point for us to understand fully that we have the power within us to decide—to *predetermine*—that we're going to live for God. That is, we can use our will to *predetermine* that we're going to set our mind on God, ahead of time. When we do that, even if we're figuratively caught off guard and drenched by five gallons of icy water, we won't start committing sin after sin after sin.

Speaking of the will, we get to determine whether our own is connected to God or to the enemy. We are given the will to decide and the will to act. God's will is always perfect, and to better hone ours, we can look more into the love that motivates His. The first time we see God's act of will in a personal way is in creation. He desired to create a universe and a world conducive to beings that He could be in relationship with, that he could call His children. His will was also for man to have a helper:

And the LORD God said, "It is not good that man should be alone; I will make him a helper comparable to him."

—Genesis 2:18

This is the first biblical reference to God having a will associated with His very personal attention toward humanity. His will was fleshed out when He created the first woman— a helper suitable for the first man. He fashioned her with His own hands, putting all the right enzymes and hormones into her body. The Creator constructed her physiology in the exact way that He predetermined for it to be. He crafted her emotionally to correspond to Him emotionally.

When God created woman, He made her with everything she'd need to fulfill her purpose on earth: Wisdom to make good choices, beauty inside and out, strength to endure challenges, compassion for those in need, and creativity to bring innovation to the world, just to name a few.

God made a choice of His will to do this. And what He did was good. In fact, God's will is always toward good.

He has a soul, a mind, and emotions. God laughs. God has joy. God weeps. We must also always remember that His will is infinitely higher than ours (Isaiah 55:9). As human beings, our will is often plagued by sin and flawed thinking. However, we can look to God as our perfect example and seek to align our will with His.

Also, each person of the Godhead has an expression of will—of choice. Jesus made the choice to give His life and die. He exercised His will so that you and I wouldn't have to suffer eternally for the choices that we've made with our will.

THE REAL YOU FULLY ALIVE

The Holy Spirit exercised His will to rest upon people in Jerusalem while celebrating the Festival of Pentecost. And just think of how all of creation came into being. God spoke it. He willed it when He said, "Let there be light," and light appeared (Genesis 1:3).

Let's go to another verse:

> *For David, after he had served his own generation by the will of God, fell asleep, was buried with his fathers, and saw corruption....*
>
> *—Acts 13:36*

In this verse, Luke the physician, inspired by the Holy Spirit, was referring to King David. We all know that David did a few stupid things in his life, things that were far more foolish than what I did that night I was drenched by a coworker.

Even though David made some terrible choices, he had a heart for God. Once he aligned his will with the Lord, he served and honored God's people for the rest of his life. That's what he's remembered for, not his poor choices, as Dr. Luke pointed out in Acts 13:36.

I've got good news. Even if you've made some careless mistakes, *you* are not a mistake. Even if you've made some atrocious choices, you don't have to continue making more of them.

We can choose, with our will, to live for God. Today can be the day we determine to set our will toward God, so that our mind and emotions don't always succeed at leading us to

CHOICES OF THE WILL

an awful, miserable place. We can make the determination to follow through on this decision. We can *predetermine* it.

You made the choice today to read this book—that was a good choice. You've possibly made the choice to go to church on a Sunday morning to be in God's house with God's people, honoring and blessing Him—that would be another good choice.

These choices come from thoughts. Yet, often, when we have a thought, it immediately transitions to emotion, and then emotion immediately leads to bodily action.

Negative thoughts don't come from God; they come from our own frustrations. When we follow those thoughts, our will is left out of the equation. Why? Because we're no longer making choices that align us with God; we're blindly following the choice the enemy is leading us to make.

By now we can better see the importance of predetermining to set our minds ahead of time. This way, when temptation comes—and it always does—we can choose, with our will, to walk with the Spirit of God.

WWJD?

In the 1990s, WWJD bracelets took the world by storm and have since become an iconic symbol of faith. It's interesting to see how one small accessory can have such a profound impact. Of course, the impact has nothing to do with the ornamental band itself, but in the timeless message.

WWJD is a powerful motto. The simple question—*what would Jesus do?*—can get our thoughts back on track, back to thinking about the love and kindness Jesus would show in a particular situation. In tough times, we can reflect on the question and recall our commitment to a moral duty, guiding our actions to demonstrate our love of Jesus. The WWJD wristbands remind us to align our will with our spirit, which should be aligned with God's Spirit, preventing our thoughts and emotions from leading us toward actions we might regret later. It's a simple reminder that helps us stay focused on what's truly important in life.

When we make a predetermination ahead of time, our thoughts will more easily align with the Spirit. However, when we let our emotions run the show, they can run rampant. We hurt people, and those people, in turn, hurt us. Behind us, we leave a trail of carnage.

We are God's sons and daughters (2 Corinthians 6:18). We can live a blessed and abundant life. We can live in a place of victory, overcoming everything the world throws at us (Romans 8:37). We don't have to be always crushed under the burdens of life. By exercising our will in harmony with the Spirit, we become stronger, preventing our emotions and thoughts from making us weaker.

We can see how it is indeed possible to live with our will connected to God's. One way to do that is by saying aloud, "Lord, help me strengthen my will in You. Help my choices get stronger in You. I no longer want my will to be absent. I no longer want my emotions leading the way in my life, making dreadful decisions and doing rotten things with my body. Lord, let my will always connect with You and be submitted to Your Spirit."

Why say something like that to the Lord? Because then we'll be able to better serve the Lord. Believe me, this kind of life is a blessed life to live. Living connected to God and serving the Lord—there's nothing that compares to it. Good choices (what I often call God choices) keep things going well in your mind.

Okay, now it's time to get practical. In the rest of this chapter, we'll review two straightforward steps that will help you strengthen your alignment with the Spirit. These tips have been instrumental in my life, and I'm positive that they'll transform your life as well.

PRACTICAL STEP #1: ASK GOD FOR WISDOM

> *If any of you lacks wisdom, let him ask of God, who gives to all liberally and without reproach, and it will be given to him. But let him ask in faith, with no doubting, for he who doubts is like a wave of the sea driven and tossed by the wind. For let not that man suppose that he will receive anything from the Lord; he is a double-minded man, unstable in all his ways.*
>
> *—James 1:5–8*

In other words, ask for wisdom in faith.

Have you ever known people who never stop bouncing all over the place in life? An entrepreneur regularly pivoting her business strategy. A college student repeatedly switching his major. A traveler always on the move, never living in one place for too long. They never seem to be content with a stable routine. It's exhausting just watching them!

A lot of problems boil down to a wisdom problem.

Academic wisdom may be in excess, but reading Wikipedia on your laptop in bed, listening to podcasts at the gym, or scrolling through social media while in the bathroom—this is not the kind of wisdom that people really need. God's wisdom is what we need. We need our will to be strong and connected to the Spirit so that we can make right choices.

So, simply ask for wisdom. Just ask for it. Open your hands and say, "God, would You give me wisdom? I want to be strong. I want to live for You, and I want my will to connect with Your Spirit. Lord, give me wisdom." After you've asked for it, trust that He will empower you to have a strong will in the Spirit.

He who has an ear, let him hear what the Spirit says....
—Revelation 2:7

God's wisdom will help keep us aligned with Him. What a comfort to know that the Holy Spirit will speak God's wisdom to us if we ask!

PRACTICAL STEP #2: ASK GODLY PEOPLE FOR COUNSEL

Proverbs is full of people asking godly individuals for advice. Here's one example:

Where there is no counsel, the people fall; but in the multitude of counselors there is safety.
—Proverbs 11:14

I'd like to tell you about one of my children and his new bride. The only way I could get permission to write this little story about them was if I agreed to include the following note, so here it is:

Josiah, you're my favorite son, and Rikki, you're my favorite daughter-in-love.

Okay! With that out of the way, here's what happened.

After my son and his then-girlfriend dated for a while, they broke up. Before getting back together, they realized they wanted to avoid hurting each other like they had the last time. So, they sought God's wisdom.

The next few steps happened quickly. Back in love, check. Engaged, check. Married, check. But at every step along the way to holy matrimony, they sought wise counsel.

At their wedding, what blessed me the most was being told by numerous people that Josiah had asked them for counsel. Each time someone mentioned that to me, I felt a little stunned, partly because my son is a man of few words. Also because—praise the Lord—both he and his future wife, Rikki, actively sought and received a *bunch* of wise counsel. That unquestionably helped them to make good choices. Ultimately, I think they made God's choice for each other, in large part because of the wise counsel they received on navigating a Christ-centered marriage.

Seeking godly counsel doesn't apply only to marital advice. We all should seek wisdom from trustworthy believers. When we put God first—above our feelings and emotions—both can be directed by, and centered upon, Christ. That means that our love, our marriage, and our day-to-day choices can be led by godly counsel and the inner wisdom of the Holy Spirit.

"I WILL" DECLARATIONS

To fully embrace the abundance that comes with walking a godly path, it's essential to know what we're able to claim in this life. We are children of the most high God—meaning, we can claim every promise He speaks over us, and we can boldly stand and proclaim life and wisdom over our own lives.

The Bible contains many "I will" statements. If you've never searched through your Bible software for them, I highly recommend it.

I've picked a few "I will" statements and listed them below. So, as we approach the end of this chapter, I invite you to stand to your feet and read the following statements aloud. You read that right. If you're reading this book on the couch in your living room, in a hammock in your backyard, or on a bench at your place of work, I encourage to stand up as you read the following verses aloud:

I will praise the LORD according to His righteousness....

—Psalm 7:17

I will praise You, O LORD, with my whole heart; I will tell of all Your marvelous works. I will be glad and rejoice in You; I will sing praise to Your name, O Most High.

—Psalm 9:1–2

I will rejoice in Your salvation.

—Psalm 9:14

I will sing to the LORD, because He has dealt bountifully with me.

—Psalm 13:6

I will love You, O LORD, my strength.

—Psalm 18:1

I will call upon the LORD, who is worthy to be praised....

—Psalm 18:3

Do you remember my story about Fred, Ron, and Ron's wife? Out front of Ron's house, I yelled, "You need to know that, for the rest of your lives, you're never going to be safe!" Well, there's more to the story.

Years after that incident, I was invited to preach at a youth service at a little town near my hometown. So, there I was, preaching at that church, and guess who was in the audience? Ron—the prankster who threw water on me—and his wife were sitting right there in front of me.

After the sermon, I approached them and instantly asked, "Am I forgiven?" Thankfully, they said, "Yeah, you're forgiven."

With Jesus, we find forgiveness and grace. Yet, our choices still have consequences: the choices we make are the choices that make us. To experience abundant life, let us choose wisely!

Chapter Four Questions

Question: What is a decision that you regret making? How might a predetermination of the will have helped you in that situation?

_____

_____

_____

_____

_____

_____

_____

_____

_____

_____

Question: In what areas of your life have worldly wisdom and your own thoughts and feelings not been enough to lead you to the right choices? How can you begin seeking God's wisdom today?

_____

_____

_____

_____

_____

_____

_____

_____

_____

_____

Question: In what ways might the counsel of godly people be beneficial in your walk with Christ? If you were to begin discussing matters of faith and God's plan for your life with another Christian, whom would you ask?

_____

_____

_____

_____

_____

_____

_____

_____

_____

_____

_____

Action: For one week, keep the "What would Jesus do?" question at the forefront of your mind to help you exercise your will to stay connected to the indwelling Spirit and respond with the wisdom and goodness of God in your decisions. As you go through the week, take note of the choices you make as a result of seeking God's will. What does your life look like at the end of this week compared to the beginning of the week?

Chapter Four Notes

Can We Trust Our Emotions?

In previous chapters, we've explored our three parts: spirit, soul, and body. We've also investigated two of the three parts of our soul: our mind and our will. This chapter dives into the third part of our soul, our emotions.

Emotions are a part of your soul, just as they are a part of God's soul. Whether we want to admit it or not, we're all emotional beings, created in the image of God, who also experiences a range of emotions. He laughs. He cries. He can be quenched and also grieved. Like Him, we are emotional beings.

Many of us are identified by our emotional tendencies. Consider the following joke:

One night, a wife finds her husband standing beside their baby's crib. As he looks down at the sleeping infant, she silently watches a mixture of emotions on her husband's face: disbelief, delight, astonishment, and skepticism. Touched by this unusual display of emotions, she slips her arm around her husband and says, "A penny for your thoughts."

"It's amazing!" he replies. "I just can't see how anybody can make a crib like that for only $150."

To me, this fun little joke reveals two things: one, the husband is probably overinvesting emotionally in things that aren't particularly important. Two, the wife isn't that adept at reading her husband's emotions. I can see myself in both of these people. Can you?

We all have an abundance of emotions. Yet, can we really trust them? What role are emotions supposed to play in our lives, and how important are they? When should we give in to our emotions, and why?

To start this exploration off right, I'd like you to ponder a few questions about yourself: What makes you cry? What makes you worry or become angry? What brings you joy or makes you laugh?

Emotions move us. Yet, it's important for us to acknowledge that emotions have the power to move us either toward or away from something or someone.

It isn't enough merely to feel our emotions. To act according to God's will, we need to understand the power behind different emotions. Our emotions can motivate us just as easily as they can devastate us, and we need to be conscious of how different emotions impact our behaviors differently.

When I think about how fascinating our emotions are, I like to remind myself how the exact same sound can cause vastly different emotions. At the birth of your child, the sound of her crying can cause you immense happiness. Yet, three months later, that same crying sound at three in the morning can cause you intense irritation.

To farmers praying for rain, thunder rumbling in the distance would sound like music to their ears. Yet, to someone wanting to celebrate a birthday outdoors, it would mean ruined plans.

The sound of fireworks could evoke fear or the feeling of nostalgia. The sound of a phone ringing could elicit annoyance or delight.

The sound of the "Wedding March," otherwise known as the "Here Comes the Bride" song, can produce laughter, crying, and tears of joy. No kidding—at three weddings I've participated in, the playing of this song caused three different groomsmen to pass out!

The point I'm trying to make is this: emotions assign either positive or negative value to things. The important question is, are our emotions bringing us down or lifting us up?

It's important for us to know that our emotional responses can make us weaker, bring us down, and take us away from God. They can also make us stronger, lift us up, and bring us closer to God.

To fully examine these principles, we're now going to explore four emotions. Two of these emotions—anxiety and discouragement—should make us wary. They're works of the flesh, so they're not part of the real *you*, who belongs to God. The other two—joy and peace—should be pursued. They're works of the Spirit, and they are part of the real you.

95

ANXIETY

Anxiety is an emotion from a world that's trying to harm us, and the enemy is often working behind this feeling.

To illuminate how God wants us to handle anxiety, we'll look at John 14:1 and explore the word *heart*, which refers to our emotions. Jesus spoke the words of this verse near the end of His life on earth as He was eating His last meal with His disciples.

Jesus had been informed by the Holy Spirit that He would soon suffer and die. He already knew that the next day He would be unjustly tried, convicted, persecuted, and crucified. Still, Jesus wanted to address the emotional state and needs of His disciples so that they could make it through that night and the rest of their lives. Now, with all of that in mind, let's read the following verse:

> *Let not your heart be troubled; you believe in God, believe also in Me.*
>
> *—John 14:1*

In that verse, the word *troubled* means "to be stirred up, to be agitated, and to become anxious."[11] Jesus knew that later that night and the next day, the disciples were going to be hit with anxiety. He needed to help them ahead of time by showing them how to hold on to God and remain confident in His goodness.

In a way, Jesus was saying, "Guys, some difficult stuff is going to happen tonight, and it might cause you to become anxious. However, I want you to hold on to your faith, stand firm, and overcome the crazy stuff that's about to happen."

Anxiety can be very destructive, and Americans are getting more and more anxious every year. According to the Anxiety and Depression Association of America, around 40 million American adults over the age of eighteen are affected by anxiety.[12] According to a 2022 Gallup poll, 42 percent of Americans said that they had experienced a lot of worry the previous day.[13]

Many of our youth struggle with anxiety, and many of them struggle with it alone, too afraid to talk about it or seek help. Every year, millions of new prescriptions for antianxiety medications are written.

I don't judge anyone who takes medication to combat anxiety. I've taken it myself. At one point in my life, I was afraid that if I fell asleep, I'd never wake up.

As mentioned in my introduction, in 2018 I went in for a simple procedure that resulted in extreme complications which almost took my life. I slipped into a coma, and the doctors put me on life support.

This was after a particularly challenging time in my life when, during a minor surgery, my bladder ruptured, causing my kidneys, spleen, pancreas, and liver to fail. I slipped into a coma, and the doctors put me on life support.

Long story short, it wasn't my time to die yet, and I eventually came out of the coma, recovered, and went home. Mind you, I was taking thirty-one prescriptions at the time, and it was definitely a struggle to stay connected to the *real* me and regain my health. All of that contributed to my fear of falling asleep, so I took anxiety medication on top of it all. That's just one reason I hold no judgment toward people who use medication to address their anxiety.

Remember, anxiety is often sent by the world, or by the enemy, to harm us. If anxiety hits you, I want you to know that you are not alone!

There was a pastor in a city near me, who fell into sin by committing adultery. When church leadership found out, they immediately dismissed him and informed him that details would be announced publicly the following day. Wrecked with anxiety, the pastor made a permanent decision based upon a temporary pain he was feeling, and he killed himself.

Regardless of whether you agree with the church's determination to make the pastor's infidelity public, the anxiety caused by his sin and their decision was very real. However, taking your life is never the answer, and it's happening way too frequently in our world. To this day, I still battle anxiety, but God is a God of hope, and a permanent decision can never solve a temporary emotion.

If you're feeling anxious about something and are considering suicide, let God help you. You might consider connecting with a suicide hotline because they are available 24 hours a day and are skilled at handling these crises. You can also go to your local church and ask fellow believers to stand with you in prayer and support. With God, better things are coming. Many faith-based and Christian counselors are trained in trauma therapy, as well. Scripture teaches us that we can overcome (Romans 8:37), and help is available. All the disciples were able to do it, and I believe you and I can, too. Let me also say that turning everything in your life over to God is a testimony that the real you is leading the way. Know this: nothing is impossible with God.

DISCOURAGEMENT

Discouragement is a deeply overwhelming emotion from the world, with the sole intention of harming us.

Beware, brethren, lest there be in any of you an evil heart of unbelief in departing from the living God....

—Hebrews 3:12

Unbelief, or doubt, is essentially the root that sprouts discouragement and all other branches of pessimism. We get tricked into believing that it's okay to walk in discouragement because everyone struggles with it. Yet, right there in Hebrews 3:12, it says that unbelief is evil. We have to keep in mind that if we allow and embrace discouragement, we'll drift further away from God and those who love us.

Many things can cause us to experience this emotion: tragedy, hard times, an unexpected death, the loss of a job, or even a broken relationship. The enemy uses discouragement to try to break us down.

Yet, as Christ followers, we can find comfort in knowing that we're more than just our soul—more than our mind, will, and emotions. We have the Spirit of God dwelling within us. We have access and connection to the Creator of the heavens and the earth. We can cling to Him and say,

"Lord, help me," which is one of the best prayers we can ever pray because it's one that He will always answer.

I still get discouraged from time to time, and I'll feel myself drifting away from God. I wake up every day wanting to achieve a lot of wonderful things for God, but occasionally I feel that progress is not happening fast enough. As a result, I become dispirited. When that happens, I think to myself, *Okay, God, okay,* and I try to listen to whether He wants me to speed up, slow down, or do something else.

We all get disheartened at times, but what do we do with the discouragement? First of all, we don't have to receive every emotion we feel. We don't have to hang on to that emotion for dear life and never let go of it. Some emotions aren't made for us to receive. They're made for us to be aware of but not to embrace.

Don't say to yourself, *I'm just a discouraged person.* No. Say to yourself, *I'm a child of God, and He doesn't give me discouragement.*

God doesn't want you to be anxious, and He doesn't want you to worry. When those emotions start spiraling you downward, that's when the real you, led by the Spirit, can capture the emotions, redeem them, and use them to take you to a positive place.

It's easy to think that we should hold on to every emotion that visits us. Some emotions are worth keeping, yes, but not all of them. Some of them should be pushed away so that we can hold on to the goodness of God. That's how much our God loves us.

Joy

Now let's talk about two emotions that we are to hold on to and value: joy and peace.

Joy is an emotion from God intended to heal us, and one way to experience it is through worship. We see this in action in Paul's letter to the Ephesians:

> *And do not be drunk with wine, in which is dissipation; but be filled with the Spirit, speaking to one another in psalms and hymns and spiritual songs, singing and making melody in your **heart** to the Lord....*
>
> **—Ephesians 5:18–19** *(emphasis mine)*

These verses highlight several expressions of God's joy. Worldly fixes, in contrast, are temporary. I find it interesting that the reference to being drunk is placed right there in the same sentence that describes the origin of real joy. Band-Aid fixes do not provide joy; only the Lord provides lasting peace and joy.

"Making melody" describes an emotional response, an act of joyfulness. Temporary pleasures can't offer the emotional fulfillment in joy that God provides for you. It's an awesome thing to receive, live in, walk in, and embrace God's joy. It moves you closer to Him. Joy will always bring you strength. How do I know? Well, here it is in the Bible:

> *You will show me the path of life; in Your presence is fullness of joy; at Your right hand are pleasures forevermore.*
>
> **—Psalm 16:11**

When we read the Psalms, we see that King David experienced some emotional ups and downs. His soul, just like ours, had high and low points, yet here we see him embracing the joy of the Lord.

> *And my soul shall be joyful in the LORD; it shall rejoice in His salvation.*
>
> **—Psalm 35:9**

I find strength in that verse. Notice that King David chose for his soul to be joyful in the Lord's presence. This reminds us that we all choose which emotions we allow to reside in our minds and in our lives.

In the Bible, hundreds of scriptures include the words *joy*, *joyful*, or *joyous*. Why? Because joy is a blessed emotion given to us from God Himself!

Joy can be yours!

PEACE

Peace is another emotion from God intended to sustain us and bring us closer to Him. In the Greek, the word is *eirēnē*. The literal meaning is "to put calm on the storm."[14] Here's a verse about peace that I love:

> *And let the peace of God rule in your hearts, to which also you were called in one body; and be thankful.*
>
> **—Colossians 3:15**

In this verse, the word *rule* means "to umpire."[15] God's peace can be the umpire, the regulator, the controller of your life, from beginning to end.

The word *hearts* means emotions.[16] So, this scripture is essentially saying to let the peace of God rule your emotions, and that's exactly what we should do. We should let God's peace set the pace for everything else in our lives.

If you struggle to give thanks, then it'll be hard for you to have joy and peace. However, if you remain thankful, it'll be easier for you to stay in the emotions God gives to bless and strengthen your life. You just have to be thankful. All the time, I encourage people to be thankful. Why? Because I've learned it myself. An attitude of gratitude can make a difference like nothing else can.

The Bible contains hundreds of references to peace! Here are three of my favorites:

I will both lie down in peace, and sleep; for You alone, O Lord, make me dwell in safety.

—Psalm 4:8

The Lord will give strength to His people; the Lord will bless His people with peace.

—Psalm 29:11

Depart from evil and do good; seek peace and pursue it.

—Psalm 34:14

Peace is an emotion from God that will help you stay centered through trials. When experiencing difficulties, instead of thinking you're alone, use God's peace to keep you moving through your troubles. It's an emotion that you will want to embrace.

We've explored two emotions (anxiety and discouragement) that are not the real you because they're from the flesh and the world, and we've examined two emotions (joy and peace) that *are* the real you because they come from God. Now let's consider some practical pointers that will help us to control all of our emotions.

TAKING CHARGE OF YOUR EMOTIONS

You might think it's okay for your emotions to rule you because perhaps you were taught by somebody who is ruled by their emotions. However, the Spirit of God should rule our life, not our feelings.

That way, we can enjoy the blessings that He has for us, and we won't always be prey to emotional outbursts. We won't be shackled by anxiety and discouragement. We'll be able to choose joy and peace.

So, where does taking charge of your emotions come from? It comes out of the following verse:

Finally, brethren, whatever things are true, whatever things are noble, whatever things are just, whatever things are pure, whatever things are lovely, whatever things are of good report, if there is any virtue and if there is anything praiseworthy—meditate on these things.

—Philippians 4:8

How do you have a blessed soul? By having blessed emotions. You can choose to meditate—to set your mind on—the things of God. Let Him, not your feelings, be on the throne of your life. You determine where your mind stays. It's easier said than done, but it is possible with a couple of key steps.

PRACTICAL STEP #1: IDENTIFY YOUR EMOTIONAL TRIGGERS

Why do certain things make us respond emotionally? Well, they're triggers. They're things, words, or actions that set us off. Know this: just because something triggered you before and took you toward darkness, it doesn't have to trigger you the next time.

To get to the heart of this idea, reread Philippians 4:8 above and answer the following question: If someone has ever lied about you, did you respond emotionally?

When we face personal injustice, such as lies told about us or hurtful words said to us, we can be triggered into an emotional response.

However, we don't need to react to those emotional triggers in ways that cause us to sin. Instead, we can recognize the triggers, then step back from them.

When I read Philippians 4:8, the message I get is *don't let the triggers take you away; let them cause you to pray.* In other words, when something difficult tempts you to say or do something you don't want to, recognize that as a trigger. Choose to hold on to and meditate on the goodness of God. Then, embrace the opposite of what the trigger is trying to get you to say or do.

For instance, if someone's lying about you, you can think to yourself, *They can lie about me, but I'm not a liar. I'm true because Jesus is the truth (John 14:6), and I love Him. He is the way for my life.*

A prominent example of a destructive emotion in my life—and perhaps yours, too—happens when I'm driving. I'll occasionally find myself trapped behind a car that's going way below the speed limit in the passing lane. Every fiber in my body wants to yell at the driver to hurry up! But how would yelling at a stranger bring glory to God? It wouldn't, of course.

So, I turn those moments of road rage into moments of grace. I continue driving slowly behind them, taking deep breaths and reminding myself to be patient. I try to shift my focus away from the frustration and, instead, cultivate a mindset of compassion and understanding.

By choosing to respond with grace, I can practice humility and recognize that I am not the center of the universe—God is.

PRACTICAL STEP #2: ESTABLISH THE HOLY SPIRIT AS THE LEADER OF YOUR EMOTIONS

Before getting married, I had a problem with lust. I had heard that lust would dissipate after marriage. Nope. That didn't happen for me, anyway. Even during my marriage, lust occasionally came after me.

Crying, I opened up to my wife about this, and Dawn committed to helping me with it. A week later at the mall, she busted me checking out a gorgeous woman. What did my brilliant wife do? She pinched me hard underneath my bicep! She squeezed me right there on what I call the *hangy down* part of my arm! Ha!

Dawn said, "Do I need to pray for you right now?"

I nodded.

She steered me away from the woman, and we prayed together. I re-established the Holy Spirit as the leader over my emotions.

As I wrote in a previous chapter, everything starts with a thought. With that in mind—pun intended—remember that thoughts don't automatically have to plunge you into negative emotions that can lead you to potentially hurtful words or actions.

In the middle of a heated discussion, you definitely shouldn't think something like, *If he says or does that, I'm going to lecture and punish him so badly that I'll leave his head spinning.* That kind of thinking will take you away from God, and that's absolutely not the person you want to be. It's not the *real* you.

Instead, in the middle of your disagreement with someone, you could think, *If he says or does that, I'm not going to respond like I did last time. Instead, I'm going to step back and thank God for the blessings He has placed in my life.* Yes, that kind of thinking will bring you closer to God, and that's exactly the person you want to be. That's the real you.

If you feel yourself leaning away from God instead of toward Him, I encourage you to pray, "Lord, I'm thinking things I shouldn't be thinking. I want to do things that I know I shouldn't do. Would You help me?" And He will.

When God helps you, you won't use your body to respond emotionally. You won't use your words and actions—all that huffing and puffing—to try to hurt someone. You will be able to live in blessing, which is precisely what God wants for you.

Chapter Five Questions

Question: What are some ways you can differentiate between emotions that are driven by the enemy and those that are genuinely inspired by the Holy Spirit?

_____

_____

_____

_____

_____

_____

_____

_____

_____

Question: In addition to the emotions of joy and peace, what other emotions can help you to discern God's will?

_____

_____

_____

_____

_____

_____

_____

_____

_____

Question: What is one permanent decision you made in the past that was a futile attempt to overpower a temporary emotion? If you could go back to that moment, what would you do differently?

_____

_____

_____

_____

_____

_____

_____

_____

_____

_____

_____

Action: Over the course of a week, intentionally assess the role your emotions play in your life. What emotions do you experience in different situations, and how do they affect your behavior? Which emotions tend to move you away from God, and which ones tend to bring you closer to Him? For each emotion that leads you away from God, determine how you will transform it into an emotion that draws you toward Him so that you will be prepared the next time you encounter a situation that triggers it.

Chapter Five Notes

Your Body: God's Temple

Our body includes all our physical attributes and our entire physical nature.[17] In this chapter, we'll explore our bodies through the lens of Scripture and identify four steps for empowering us to use them in ways that add to our spiritual life, instead of subtracting from it.

Before we go to be with God forever, we will be given an account of all the good and bad things we did with our bodies:

> *For we must all appear before the judgment seat of Christ, that each one may receive the things done in the body, according to what he has done, whether good or bad.*
>
> *—2 Corinthians 5:10*

This verse is crucial because it shows us how important our bodies are to God. One day, when we stand before God, and He asks us how we used our bodies, we'll be accountable for two things: every idle word we've said and every deed we've done.

I like to call our bodies "earth suits" because they will change dramatically when we move from here to heaven. At that moment, our temporary bodies will be made perfect. All our physical flaws will be transformed, and we will experience full restoration. This is a beautiful promise that we can hold on to. We can look forward to a place where there is perfection—no pain and no suffering. In this new place, our bodies will never perish, and we'll be in the presence of God forever (Revelation 21:4).

Here on earth, however, as a spirit who possesses a soul and lives in a body, you can learn many wonderful things from Scripture about your body, God's temple (1 Corinthians 6:19).

Before we get into all that weighty stuff, let's start this chapter off with some lighthearted humor. After all, there are so many funny jokes out there about our bodies.

What did the skeleton order for dinner? Spare ribs!

Why can't a nose be twelve inches long? Because then it would be a foot!

What did the left hand say to the right hand? "Why do you always get to be right?"

With those laughs—or groans—out of the way, I'd like to ask a few important questions: How is your body doing? Does your body help or hinder your spiritual life? Does your body move you toward or away from God?

Here's my most important question for you: How can you ensure that your body helps you spiritually?

STEP #1: PRESENT YOUR BODY TO GOD

I beseech you therefore, brethren, by the mercies of God, that you present your bodies a living sacrifice, holy, acceptable to God, which is your reasonable service.

—Romans 12:1

How do we conduct our life? We do it with and through our body. In other words, our body is the vessel for our life. Reading this verse, we see that it should be a natural act of service for us to use our bodies as a blessing to God.

Let's read the next verse so we can better understand this concept:

And do not be conformed to this world, but be transformed by the renewing of your mind, that you may prove what is that good and acceptable and perfect will of God.

—Romans 12:2

Your body belongs to God; you're just its temporary caretaker. Have you ever *presented your body* to God? I frequently present my body to God, aligned with the spiritual armor He gives us to wear. I find this to be a useful way to ask God to help me with my body.

Therefore take up the whole armor of God, that you may be able to withstand in the evil day, and having done all, to stand. Stand therefore, having girded your waist with truth, having put on the breastplate of righteousness, and having shod your feet with the preparation of the gospel of peace; above all, taking the shield of faith with which you will be able to quench all the fiery

115

darts of the wicked one. And take the helmet of salvation, and
the sword of the Spirit, which is the word of God....

—Ephesians 6:13-17

Did you notice the above references to a belt, breastplate, shoes ("feet fitted"), a shield, and a helmet? Well, here's how I physically act out those verses with my body.

First, I wrap my hands around me like I'm putting on an invisible belt, which symbolizes the belt of truth. I pray, "Lord, would You help me so that only truth happens here and no untruth takes root?"

Second, I wrap my hands around my upper waist like I'm putting on an invisible breastplate, symbolizing the breastplate of righteousness. I pray, "Lord, as I put this on, would You help me to think and do right things with my body?"

Next, I use my hands to put on a pair of invisible shoes. These are the gospel sandals of peace. I pray, "Lord, wherever my feet take me, would You let peace arrive there as well?"

Then, I raise my hands over my head as though I'm putting on an invisible helmet, the helmet of salvation. I pray, "Lord, would You cause my brain to work the way You want it to work?"

After donning the helmet, I lift one of my arms to hold my invisible shield of faith. I pray, "Lord, would You help me to think and act with full confidence in Your goodness and complete faith everywhere I go?"

Lastly, I wield an invisible sword with my other hand. This is the sword of the Spirit. I pray, "Lord, would You cause the truth of Your Word to flow from me today?"

I fully believe that we can present our bodies to God. I encourage you to do it if you've never tried. If the way I present my body seems a bit too cumbersome, then instead of doing all the above motions, you could simply say, "Lord, all of my body—the good and the bad—is Yours. It's all going to be used for You!"

STEP #2: STOP DOING ANYTHING THAT HARMS YOUR BODY

Why should you refrain from harming your body? Because your body is the temple of God.

Do you not know that you are the temple of God and that the Spirit of God dwells in you?

—1 Corinthians 3:16

I'd like to draw a parallel between your body, which is currently God's temple, and the temple in Jerusalem.

The temple was renowned for its grandeur and architectural beauty. It was constructed using white stones, adorned with intricate carvings, and covered with gold and other precious materials. The massive outer walls featured ornate gates and covered walkways. People donated linen, silk, gold, silver, and other beautiful things to the temple so that it would bring honor and glory to God.

The innermost chamber of the temple housed the ark of the covenant, inside which were the two stone tablets inscribed with the Ten Commandments. This sacred chamber

117

was separated from the rest of the temple by a thick curtain, symbolizing the separation between the divine and the mortal realms.

Most of the temple was later destroyed. The only thing left standing was the footing on the west side called the Wailing Wall, or the Western Wall. Before it was destroyed, the temple was undeniably incredible. As it might be said, it was off-the-charts awesome. If the temple was built in modern times, it would cost hundreds of billions of dollars.

The Bible says right there in 1 Corinthians 3:16 that you are now the temple of God. You are now where God's Spirit dwells. You are, if you will, a living, breathing temple that should be in some way similar to the temple that was in Jerusalem.

> *If anyone defiles the temple of God, God will destroy him. For the temple of God is holy, which temple you are.*
>
> **—1 Corinthians 3:17**

In this verse, the word *defile* means "to corrupt."[18] The point is that God doesn't want us to corrupt or harm our bodies.

> *Or do you not know that your body is the temple of the Holy Spirit who is in you, whom you have from God, and you are not your own? For you were bought at a price; therefore glorify God in your body and in your spirit, which are God's.*
>
> **—1 Corinthians 6:19–20**

In other words, let your body be something that gives God glory, something that causes Him to receive honor. You never want your body to affect your spirit adversely. To put it as plainly as I possibly can: don't harm yourself; rather, help yourself.

Abuse of caffeine, alcohol, or drugs, even overeating or undereating, causes harm to your body, and illicit sexual activity defiles God's temple. Do things that bring you joy and peace, but don't cross the line into self-sabotage. Where is that line? The Holy Spirit will show you if you ask.

One way to do this is to pray and give your harmful practices to the Lord. Another approach is to make the choice and say to yourself, *I am not going to harm what God Himself died for. Jesus gave His life so that our bodies could be resurrected and we could have His life in us now. The Bible tells us that we are where His presence dwells. I shouldn't dare harm this body, this temple.*

STEP #3: STAY ACTIVE TO KEEP YOUR BODY FROM LIMITING YOUR SPIRIT

I sourced this step from a passage of Scripture in which the Apostle Paul instructs his young pastor friend Timothy:

> But reject profane and old wives' fables, and exercise yourself toward godliness. For bodily exercise profits a little, but godliness is profitable for all things, having promise of the life that now is and of that which is to come.
>
> **—1 Timothy 4:7–8**

119

Even though Paul was teaching about godliness, he still pointed out that exercise is profitable and helpful for the body. Indeed, the word *exercise* appears multiple times in the Bible. Jesus exercised. He walked everywhere. He also worked hard labor as a carpenter.

As a Roman citizen, Paul might have attended the Olympic Games and witnessed firsthand how devoted the athletes were to their bodies. Perhaps that's when Paul conceived the parallel between working out our bodies and working out our godliness. If we're disciplined in both, then our bodies won't hold back our spirits.

Part of staying healthy is making sure that we don't go to extremes with our bodies. Bodily neglect is a sin, just as bodily worship is. Balance is the key. I've seen people neglect their bodies, and I've seen people worship their bodies. Both extremes are ungodly. God wants us to land somewhere in the middle, where we're not short-circuiting our lives and our purpose by neglecting our physical health but also not obsessing over our outward appearance and physical strength.

I know there are aspects of my physical health that I can affect positively or negatively, so I stretch and lift weights. I do strength work and general fitness work. I exercise because I don't want my body to hold back my spirit. If my body is not functioning at an optimal level, neither will my spirit. We are holistic beings, and abuse or neglect of one part will inevitably result in the downfall of the rest.

Are you willing to help your body do better? Could you hike through the mountains or swim in the ocean, all the while reminding yourself of the power and awesomeness of

God's creation all around us? Could you pedal on an exercise bike while listening to worship music? Could you join a sports team and meet other Christians who want to build community through exercise?

Exercising doesn't have to be complicated, but it is vital to ensuring that your body doesn't ever hold you back. Good health is a complement to an abundant life.

STEP #4: RECOGNIZE THAT YOUR BODY BELONGS TO GOD!

The lamp of the body is the eye. Therefore, when your eye is good, your whole body also is full of light. But when your eye is bad, your body also is full of darkness.

—Luke 11:34

In this verse, I find the use of *eye* rather interesting. Our minds will focus on whatever our eyes stare at, and then our bodies will pursue it. The verse makes it clear that we have a choice. We can choose to be *good*, which is healthy, or we can choose to be *bad*, which is unhealthy.

God wants you to be healthy, and there's nothing wrong with that. If you're not yet as healthy as you want to be, that's nothing to be ashamed of. God is giving you an opportunity to add to your faith by being physically healthy, so as soon as you're ready, take it!

As I've shared in previous chapters, we're all made of three parts—spirit, soul, and body—all of which are important to God, and none of which are to be neglected. That's why it's so essential to keep your body healthy and strong—because it helps your spirit and soul to also stay healthy and strong.

Our three parts are all connected. In that way, we're so much more than just our bodies. Said a little differently, we're so much more than that fun song we learned in school about anatomy, in which we sang the names of different body parts while pointing to them:

> The leg bone's connected to the knee bone.
>
> The knee bone's connected to the thigh bone.
>
> The thigh bone's connected to the hip bone. ...

We're so much more than just our bodies! When you read the following, try singing it in your mind:

> Your spirit is connected to your soul.
>
> Your soul is connected to your body.
>
> Your body is connected to your spirit.
>
> So live a blessed life!

Chapter Six Questions

Question: What does it mean to present your body as "a living sacrifice, holy, acceptable to God," and how is this "your reasonable service" (Romans 12:1)?

_____

_____

_____

_____

_____

_____

_____

_____

_____

Question: What harmful things are you currently doing to your body, and what steps will you take to turn away from those practices?

_____

_____

_____

_____

_____

_____

_____

_____

_____

_____

Question: In what ways does your body add to your spiritual life instead of taking away from it, and how will you now use your body to give glory to God and bring you closer to Him?

_____

_____

_____

_____

_____

_____

_____

_____

_____

_____

_____

_____

Action: Every day, make a point of dedicating your body to God. Point to the various parts of your temporary, decaying body and say aloud to the Lord, "These eyes, these ears, this mouth, these hands, these legs, and all the rest of my body are Yours. They are sanctified to You; use them according to Your will. Help me to honor and glorify You with my body today."

125

Chapter Six Notes

_____

_____

_____

_____

_____

_____

_____

_____

_____

_____

_____

_____

_____

_____

_____

_____

_____

_____

_____

_____

The Real You

I wrote this book for you because I want you to live a blessed, abundant life. I also want you to understand the truth about who you really are.

Thank you for staying with me through these pages. I hope and pray that what I've shared with you will bring you closer to God.

I have one final question for you. It might seem like a strange question, but for me it's quite pertinent. When someone prays for you, is there something that you regularly do with your body? For example, I like to open my hands and face my palms upward when someone prays for me as a sign to them, me, and the world that I intend to receive all the blessings of God that might be covered by the prayer. This simple gesture reveals that I'm open to receiving all that the Lord has for me through the prayer.

I'd like to pray for you now. I know that you're holding this book in your hands, so it won't be easy for you to read this last part while also holding your hands open, palms up. That said, if there's something you often do when someone prays for you, I invite you to do it now. If it's kneeling, please kneel. If it's bowing your head, please bow your head. Whatever it is, now is a great time to do it because I'd like nothing more than to end this book with a prayer just for you:

> Father in heaven, I come to You in the name of Jesus, and I want to thank You. You are the Creator of the heavens and the earth. You created me, the person reading this book, and everyone else in the world. I want to thank You, Lord, for creating us in Your image. I want to thank You for moments like this, when we turn toward You and see how good You are.
>
> Lord, I'm praying right now that, as we turn toward You, my friend reading these very words on this page and I will experience a blessing released from heaven into our minds, will, and emotions, bringing us strength.
>
> I pray, Lord God, and stand in faith against every scheme of the enemy that's trying to break my friend down. Everything of this world that's trying to quench my friend's spirit, I pray, Lord, that it would be undone right now.
>
> Lord, You are a good and gracious God, and I want to thank You for it. I pray that You would release grace right now upon the person reading this book. This I pray in Jesus' mighty name. Amen.

About the Author

Jeff Klingenberg's heart can be captured in one phrase: *strengthening people for life.* This phrase, though seemingly simple, holds deep meaning and purpose. At HighRidge Church, Jeff and his wife, Dawn, share a hope that everyone would be encouraged and become a passionate worshipper of God.

However, it does not end there. Jeff believes that individual believers must be built up in order to build others up. His desire is that HighRidge's motto will become a way of life for everyone. His prayer is that we all would live to encourage, uplift, and strengthen those around us. In this way, God's purposes will be fulfilled as the body of Christ continues to reach the world with the message of hope in Jesus Christ.

About Renown Publishing

Renown Publishing is an elite team of professionals devoted to helping you shape, write, and share your book. Renown has written, edited, and worked on hundreds of books (including New York Times, Wall Street Journal, and USA Today best-sellers, and the #1 book on all of Amazon).

We believe authentic stories are the torch of change-makers, and our mission is to collaborate with purpose-driven authors to create societal impact and redeem culture.

If you're the founder of a purpose-driven company, or an aspiring author, visit RenownPublishing.com.

Notes

1. Vine, W. E., and Merrill Unger. "G4151 – pneuma." *Vine's Complete Expository Dictionary of Old and New Testament Words: With Topical Index.* Thomas Nelson, 1996.

2. Vine and Unger, "G5590 – psyche."

3. Vine and Unger, "G4983 – soma."

4. Vine and Unger, "G1487 – ei."

5. Vine and Unger, "G1487 – ei."

6. Gibson, Mel, dir. *Braveheart.* Icon Entertainment International, 1995.

7. Vine and Unger, "G215 – alalētos."

8. Klein, Laurie. "I Love You, Lord," House of Mercy Music, 1978.

9. Sengupta, Trisha. "Dog Gets Trapped Inside Toilet with Leopard for Hours, Miraculously Survives." *Hindustan Times.* February 4, 2021. https://www.hindustantimes.com/trending/

dog-gets-trapped-inside-toilet-with-leopard-for-hours-miraculously-survives-101612438990469.html

10. Vine and Unger, "G3540 – noēma."

11. Vine and Unger, "G5015 – tarassō."

12. Anxiety and Depression Association of America. "Anxiety Disorders: Facts and Statistics." https://adaa.org/understanding-anxiety/facts-statistics.

13. Gallup. "2022 Global Emotions Report." https://www.gallup.com/analytics/349280/gallup-global-emotions-report.aspx.

14. Vine and Unger, "G1515 – eirēnē."

15. Vine and Unger, "G1018 – brabeuō."

16. Vine and Unger, "G2588 – kardia."

17. Vine and Unger, "G4983 – soma."

18. Vine and Unger, "G5351 – phtheirō."

Made in the USA
Middletown, DE
02 September 2024

60253345R10084